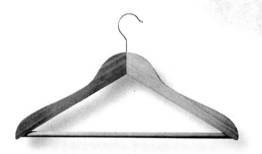

CHRISTIAN MODESTY

A Matter of the Heart

Jerry & Heidi Beaver

CHRISTIAN MODESTY
A Matter of the Heart

Copyright © 2010 by Jerry & Heidi Beaver

All Scripture quotes are from the King James Bible.

ISBN: 978-0-9827038-0-9
Published by Baptist Growth Publications
Pleasant Prairie, WI

CHRISTIAN MODESTY
A Matter of the Heart

By Jerry & Heidi Beaver

TABLE OF CONTENTS

INTRODUCTION

The pastor of a small church felt energized as he led the visiting missionary to the sanctuary. The church members had given funds over a course of several years to support this particular missionary. Today, the pastor's congregation would hear of and see images from a tribe living deep within the African jungle. They would learn of the trials of the missionary and hear stories of many wonderful conversions to Christ within the African tribe.

With excitement, the pastor helped the missionary set up a large screen and slide projector. The missionary attached the large tray of slides to the projector. The pastor dimmed the lights, as they were ready to preview a few slides to make sure the equipment worked properly.

An image of the missionary and his family flashed across the screen. The missionary, his wife, and daughters smiled back from the picture. The missionary pressed the button to advance the slides.

An image of crudely built huts with grass roofs filled the front of the sanctuary. The missionary pressed the button again and again and again. As different photos depicting the area where the missionary served came on the screen, the pastor gazed upon beautiful foliage, exotic animals, and tribal buildings that were far different from what his local congregation had experienced.

Then a slide showing men in tribal dress filled the screen. The pastor noticed the large loincloths tied around the men's waists, necklaces made from animals' teeth tied around their necks, and bright colored cloth tied around their heads. The missionary quickly pushed the button.

A picture of several tribal women overflowed from the screen. The pastor gasped. The tribal women were topless. "You're going to have to remove those slides from your presentation," he said.

The missionary looked perplexed. "Why?" he asked.

"Because some of the ladies are partially naked."

"But that is the culture in Africa," the missionary replied. "We have not gone there to change their culture, but their hearts."

The pastor nodded. "I agree, however, there is still right and wrong within any culture. Let me explain."

He asked the missionary to click the button again. The next photograph was of the missionary's wife and daughters, surrounded by several tribal women.

"Why are your wife and daughters wearing tops? Are you not trying to reach these people? If it is acceptable for the ladies in this African tribe, then it should be okay for your daughters as well."

"Well, it is different," the missionary said.

"How is it different? You said culture made it right. Is your family not living in that culture?"

"Well. . ." the missionary struggled to find words to justify his argument.

The pastor watched.

The missionary sighed, then reached forward and removed several slides from the carousel tray.[1]

I think this conversation clearly illustrates some of the problems regarding the subject of clothing and Christians. There are countless arguments on both sides of the modesty fence, and while many of them may seem logical and justified, they are not necessarily biblical. We must direct these arguments back to what God says. We must seek His answer for us, not our own answers based on personal opinion, bias, or convenience.

Our goal with this book is to inform, challenge, and prompt you by the Spirit of God to seek the Lord concerning your outward appearance and testimony. At times, this book may appear directed more toward women than men. (Honestly, I often feel bad for our ladies because they are criticized more often than men about their attire.) However, this book also instructs men about their responsibilities regarding their minds, hearts, outward adornment, and Christ-likeness. I pray that this book becomes a guide for 1) every husband and father as he leads his wife and daughters, 2) all women as they strive to live within Christian guidelines, and 3) every pastor as he upholds modesty principles in his church.

As my wife and I worked on this book, we were tempted to avoid certain issues (e.g., women wearing pants). However, too many books on the market today already neglect this area. We knew that if we followed the same writing trend, we would lose our purpose for this book.

We understand why many authors avoid the subject of Christian modesty. Many of the issues on modesty as they pertain to dress are like lightning rods, inviting readers and congregations the opportunity to criticize the author as well as the opinion. There are many varying opinions by good Christians and pastors, opinions that are often in direct conflict with one another.

Our goal in writing this book is to be honest with Scripture first, then empower the reader to look outside their culture, whether conservative, progressive, or liberal, and make a biblical decision of what is best for their testimony and the Lord.

Maybe you have never been convicted of immodesty, never heard that pants were an issue of dress for women, or don't know where to begin with dress standards for a Christian. Maybe you have no church background or a background where these issues were not discussed. We pray this book will be of service to you. We believe Christians today vitally need guidelines such as set forth in this book. Keep reading! You won't regret it.

CHAPTER ONE

Does Culture Decide What is Right or Wrong?

Brenda walked down the aisle in response to the invitation at the close of the church service, prayed, and received the Lord as her Savior. Eager to know all she could about the Lord, she was soon on fire spiritually. Over the next few weeks and months, God used her enthusiasm and obedience to bring people to church. Brenda soon saw many of her friends accept God's salvation. She wanted to do more for God and felt led to volunteer to teach a children's Sunday school class.

She approached the Sunday school director, Mr. Smith, and asked about the opportunities for serving the Lord in this capacity. Mr. Smith, who had difficulty recruiting volunteers, was excited to have someone offer to help in this much-needed area. He grinned as he quickly explained the training offered and what the job entailed. Then, his smile slid from his face as he continued. "You do realize, don't you, that there is a small detail that needs to be addressed?"

Brenda shook her head. She didn't know what Mr. Smith was referring to.

"You'll have to agree that you will not wear pants to church anymore. Furthermore, you need to make sure that when you are out in public your attire and dress is of the utmost modesty."

Brenda felt confused. She had worn pants to church since her conversion. No one had mentioned this issue to her before. The pastor had never preached on what was appropriate and inappropriate for Christian dress. Brenda had noticed the other ladies within the congregation wore dresses, but the majority of them were much older than her and she thought the choice and style of clothing had to do with the era of their upbringing. She never attributed their choice to spiritual decisions.

Growing up, Brenda had been a typical tomboy. It was hard enough to keep up with three older brothers. A skirt or dress only added to the difficulty, therefore she wore worn-out, hand-me-down jeans most of the time. She found dresses awkward and pants more to her liking.

She tried to think back to the last time she had worn a dress. Had it been her prom, her wedding, a special date with her husband? She wasn't sure. After her children were born, it had been easier to maneuver around the house in what was comfortable to her. Being a soccer mom, climbing in and out of vans, and running a household was easier in a pair of slacks. The dresses had slowly vanished from her closet.

Brenda became troubled about what the ladies in the church thought of her and her style of dress. Why hadn't someone mentioned this to her before and why would the church care if she was dressed in pants or a dress/skirt?

The following Sunday, Brenda approached an older woman in the church. "Mrs. Johnson, can you help mentor me about church attire? I don't understand the rule about women wearing dresses."

Mrs. Johnson's lips pursed into a smug smile. "I know that you're a new Christian, but the Bible says that pants are men's attire and to wear them is considered an abomination to the Lord."

Brenda's stomach contracted into a small ball. She had never wanted to be an abomination to the Lord. "I have read through the Bible three times already and I have never seen that. Can you give me the chapter and verse where God says that?"

"Certainly. It's in the book of Deuteronomy, chapter twenty-two."

Brenda jotted the Scripture reference on the front of her morning bulletin, vowing to look it up as soon as she got home. As she left the church that morning, Brenda's heart felt heavy and her spirit was lower than it had been since her conversion. "Am I an abomination to the Lord? Am I sinning by wearing pants?"

As soon as Brenda got home, she sat in her favorite chair, opened her Bible, and turned to Deuteronomy chapter twenty-two. She began at verse one. When she got to verse five, she found the word *abomination*. This must be the passage Mrs. Johnson referred to. She read it several times to herself, then aloud. "The woman shall not wear that which pertaineth unto a man, neither shall a man put on a woman's garment: for all that do so *are* abomination unto the LORD thy God" (Deuteronomy 22:5).

Brenda read the verse again and again and again. Where was the part about pants? Were pants considered men's attire? Brenda had never seen it like that. She had worn pants all her life, never thinking they were not ladylike.

Brenda's burden to teach children burned in her, and though she did not feel a conviction regarding women wearing pants, she agreed to wear dresses to church. Because of her lack of conviction, Brenda thought of herself as a hypocrite, she felt like an outcast at church, and eventually her relationship with the church suffered. She worried about her daughters growing up in this congregation. How would they be received? She made her daughters wear dresses, but she always felt as though she was putting on a show for the church ladies.

Eventually, Brenda left the church where she had been converted and began attending a church with little to no rules or pressure. The standards and convictions were loose, but at least in her new church, she was allowed to be herself. The sad thing is, because the church had no formal instructtions and guidelines for biblical living, Brenda lost her teenage daughters to the world.

In this story, who was wrong? The church? Brenda? The ladies in the church? Mr. Smith? Mrs. Johnson? The pastor? The church with no standards? The teenage daughters? Throughout this book, I will tell you why I believe they were all wrong. (Since this book is co-written, anytime the word "I" is used it is referring to Jerry.)

In Brenda's story, you could put many faces to the problem. People come from different walks of life. Brenda could just have easily been a lady accustomed to wearing skirts above her knees, shorts, or capris. It could be the story of a man with tattoos covering his body, earrings, a tongue ring, or any other fashion some Christians deem inappropriate.

I titled this chapter *Does Culture Decide What is Right or Wrong?* I started with this question for a purpose. I believe error must be exposed before truth can be digested. I am convinced that there is much error in the world and the Church concerning our outward appearance.

In answering the question, *Does Culture Decide What is Right or Wrong?* My answer is no and yes. Confusing? Yes, but hold on while I explain.

Let's go back to the garden of Eden. In the beginning, Adam and Eve only knew that which was good. Then Satan tempted Eve. He told her she could know evil and good and be as gods if she ate the fruit from a tree that God had said not to eat from. When Eve gave in to the temptation, she disobeyed God and trespassed into sin. Adam soon followed. When sin had engulfed them, their consciences awakened.

The Bible states, "And the eyes of them both were opened, and they knew that they *were* naked; and they sewed fig leaves together, and made themselves aprons" (Genesis 3:7). As I studied this Scripture, I was surprised to note that the immediate result of the first sin among mankind revealed the state of nakedness to the human conscience. This awareness caused Adam and Eve to experience shame.

In response to this humiliating new emotion, they tried to cover themselves. Their attempt was inadequate and God replaced their fig leaf aprons with animal skins. Theologians teach that this event pictures Christ's redemptive plan and blood sacrifice. However, there is no getting away from the fact that when sin came into the picture, Adam and Eve's eyes were opened and awareness of nakedness was stirred, manifesting itself in shame.

In Nancy Leigh DeMoss' booklet, *The Look: Does God Really Care What I Wear?* she says this about Adam and Eve:

> They didn't ask God's advice about how to dress. Instead, they came up with their

own plan—they sewed fig leaves together to cover their private parts. (Did you know that figs leaves have the consistency of sand paper?) . . . They quickly realized that the fig leaves couldn't adequately solve their problem, so they hid themselves.[2]

There are many examples in the Bible where Scripture addresses the subject of nakedness. When Noah lay uncovered in his tent, one of his sons, Ham, saw his nakedness and told his brothers. The brothers, Shem and Japheth, realized that their father needed to be covered. Without looking upon their father and his naked body, they walked backwards into the tent and covered Noah with a garment. When Noah awoke and found out what had happened, he cursed Ham, but blessed Shem and Japheth. (See Genesis 9:22-26.)

As we move on in the Bible, we find that after God's children escaped Egypt, and while they wandered through the wilderness, the Lord gave them laws to govern much of their lifestyle. In Leviticus chapter 18, we read where He commanded His children concerning themselves being clothed or covered in front of family and strangers, thereby keeping themselves from revealing their nakedness.

Also, in Proverbs 7:6-23 we read:

For at the window of my house I looked through my casement, And beheld among the <u>simple ones,</u> I discerned among the youths, a young man <u>void of understanding,</u> Passing through the street near her corner; and he went the way to her house, In the twilight, in the evening, in the black and dark night: And, behold, there met him a woman *with* the attire <u>of an harlot, and subtil of heart. (She is loud and stubborn;</u> her feet abide not in her house: Now is *she* without, now in the streets, and lieth in wait at every corner.) So she caught him, and kissed him, *and* with an impudent face said unto him, <u>I *have* peace offerings</u> with me; this day have I payed my vows. Therefore came I forth to meet thee, diligently to seek thy face, and I have found thee. I have decked my bed with coverings of tapestry, with carved *works*, with fine linen of Egypt. I have perfumed my bed with myrrh, aloes, and cinnamon. Come, let us take our fill of love until the morning: let us solace ourselves with loves. For the goodman is not at home, he is gone a long journey: He hath taken a bag of money with him, *and* will come home at the day appointed. With her much fair speech she caused him to yield, with the flattering of her lips she forced him. He goeth after her straightway, as an ox goeth to the slaughter, or as a fool to the correction of the stocks; Till a dart strike through his liver; as a bird hasteth to the snare, and knoweth not that it *is* for his life. (emphasis added)

I would like to point out several thoughts regarding nakedness from the previous text. First is the phrase, "void of understanding." Many times, we are void of understanding when it comes to the influence women have upon men. That influence is powerful and, at times, stronger than one may think.

Men are visual creatures. Most of them are attracted to the opposite sex by what they see. In the previous Scripture, the young man is referred to as one of the "simple" ones because he did not understand what was happening. That lack of understanding allowed him to be lured by the woman.

I believe many Christians have become "simple" when it comes to their attire. They are following the way of the world, being lured by a lack of understanding. On the other hand, there are many Christians who have gone too far to the other spectrum. They mean well and have good intentions, but their appearance is plain and unattractive. Some have the attitude that to look godly, one must look homely.

The second thought concerning nakedness from this passage of Scripture relates to the words "with the attire of an harlot." A harlot is a prostitute, a person who sells her body, using it in a sinful and degrading way. With her words, "I have peace offerings," she means to give speculation that she is a spiritual person. And once she catches this simple young man's attention with her attire and false promises, she continues, "With her much fair speech caused him to yield, with the flattering of her lips she forced him." Now, let's sum up these verses. With the "attire of an harlot" she dresses for the purpose of luring this young man. He was forced into sin because of her seductive attire.

This story from Scripture illustrates the lure of nakedness and the destructive end when it is not under the auspices of God's Word. We readily admit that one would expect a harlot to dress immodestly. As an unsaved person, she would not necessarily be convicted of the sin involved with her nakedness. But Christian women are commanded to dress with modesty.

Yes, as Christians, we are called to a higher standard. One would not expect a Christian man or woman to purposely seek to lure another person into their bedroom. However, unlike this woman in Proverbs, who knew exactly what she was doing, Christians can still lead another person into sin, and do so without knowing it.

When we read the story of David, a man after God's own heart, we see that he looked out his window and was captivated by the nakedness of Bathsheba. The vision of her lured him and eventually drove him to the point that he murdered her husband to cover up his sin. I really don't think it was the motive of Bathsheba to lure David;

however, that is precisely what she did, and it cost both of them greatly. As for David, it cost him his reputation and his family. This goes to show how serious the subject of modesty is for both men and women.

This brings me to an important principle. Because men are visually stimulated, women can tempt a man, or many men, without knowing it. Just as the harlot dresses with a purpose to lure men to her bed, Christians must dress with purpose to show godly hearts and to avoid leading one another into temptation. Whether dressing for school, work, home, or other functions, we must consciously prepare our outer appearance to be a witness of our inner testimony. The old saying goes, "Dress for success." Our exterior appearance is the first impression others have of us, thus, this is very important for Christians who are seeking to win others to Christ to refrain from being a stumbling block to others.

Unfortunately, you and I live in a wicked world with more unsaved people than saved. The media, entertainment sources, and department stores of today's culture don't cater to Christians but to the godless. This makes it difficult for Christians when choosing and buying clothing.

That brings us back to my original question. *Does Culture Decide What is Right and Wrong?* It certainly can, and in some respects, it should. Often the culture dictates what Christians should avoid. For instance, the culture of the harlot dictated her dress. A Christian woman seeing that type of attire, and knowing its association with the harlot and sinfulness, would choose to dress differently. She would make a conscious decision to adhere to the truth and dress in a manner that brought honor to God.

Christians' dress should not be dictated away from God's Word by any culture, especially when that culture is contrary to God's principles. Thus, there should be a difference in the believer's attire to show separation from ungodly values and practices.

Whether we like it or not, we are affected by our culture and, unfortunately, we live in a sinful world. Christians are not to follow the tides and fads of the world, especially when it has no shame for nakedness. A classic verse that shows the proper Christian response to the world and its rudiments is found in 2 Corinthians 6:17, "Wherefore come out from among them, and be ye separate, saith the Lord, and touch not the unclean *thing*; and I will receive you." We must remain separate from the sinful world, as 1 Peter 1:14 commands, "As obedient children, not fashioning yourselves according to the former lusts in your ignorance."

Does culture dictate what we wear? Yes, culture dictates our dress as Christians. It shows us the good and the bad. It is our duty as Christians to discern between the two and not touch the unclean things.

Growing up, I sometimes rebelled and argued with my parents. If they told me not to do something that I really wanted to do, I'd come back with the typical response, "But Johnny does it!" My parents, probably quite like yours, would respond, "Well, if Johnny jumped off a bridge, would you do it?" We all know that the expected answer is no. The fact that everyone in the world is doing something does not make it right.

Many parents shed tears of frustration. Their teenage children complain that what they have chosen to adorn themselves with is "just the style" or "everyone is wearing it" or they say, "I want to fit in!" Although the parents know that certain styles are worldly and attract the wrong kind of influences for their children, it is often easier to avoid conflict by ignoring the issue. This becomes harmful to their children's godly character. As parents, we are called to protect and instruct our children and to stand against the tides of the world for them.

Going back to our story of the missionary in the Introduction, yes, everyone in Africa may be walking around naked, but it does not make it right. When God speaks in His Word about nakedness and its sinfulness, He is adamant that men and women should be covered. In Leviticus 18:1-5, we read:

> And the LORD spake unto Moses, saying,
> Speak unto the children of Israel, and say

unto them, I am the LORD your God. After the doings of the land of Egypt, wherein ye dwelt, shall ye not do: and after the doings of the land of Canaan, whither I bring you, shall ye not do: neither shall ye walk in their ordinances. Ye shall do my judgments, and keep mine ordinances, to walk therein: I *am* the LORD your God. Ye shall therefore keep my statutes, and my judgments: which if a man do, he shall live in them: I *am* the LORD.

As seen in these last verses, God is very clear about not taking on pagan cultures. What is more interesting is the next verse: "None of you shall approach to any that is near of kin to him, to uncover *their* nakedness: I am the LORD" (Leviticus 18:6).

We see this process of separation from the world played out in the book of Genesis. When God told Jacob to go to Bethel, He gave him specific instructions: "And God said unto Jacob, Arise, go up to Bethel, and dwell there: and make there an altar unto God, that appeared unto thee when thou fleddest from the face of Esau thy brother. Then Jacob said unto his household, and to all that *were* with him, Put away the strange gods that *are* among you, and be clean, <u>and change your garments</u> (Genesis 35:1-2; emphasis added).

Pagan cultures rub off on us, and we, as Christians, have to be careful that while we are in the world, we are not of the world.

CHAPTER TWO

What Does the Bible Say about Nakedness?

As we already saw from the stories of Adam and Eve, David and Bathsheba, Jacob, and others, nakedness is sinful and was brought under the judgment of God. But what else does the Bible say about nakedness and the definition of it?

In all honesty, here lies the argument: for what may be nakedness to you may not be to me and vice versa. We know that not all nakedness is wrong, for nakedness among married couples is perfectly fine and even encouraged. (See Hebrews 13:4 and Song of Solomon.) However, outside of that context, it is to be avoided.

Why is Nakedness Outside of Marriage Sinful?

As we look again to Adam and Eve, we see that their nakedness was the first thing they realized after they sinned. They immediately tried to hide their nakedness with inadequate coverings, which God replaced with His coverings.

The first reason nakedness is sinful outside of marriage is the fact that nakedness, or the awareness of it, is a direct result of sin. God hates sin. His response was to provide coverings, which I believe concealed the private areas of both the man and the woman. (We will look at this fact more later.)

When we uncover ourselves publicly, this act represents rebellion toward God, just as Adam and Eve rebelled. Their guilt was associated with the revelation of nudity. God covered them to eliminate the visual evidence of their guilt. When we get to Heaven, we will not have to wear clothes, though we do read of people in Heaven wearing white robes. Until then, we need to keep ourselves covered because of our sinful flesh. God covered Adam and Eve in the Garden, and thus we need to stay covered today.

Second, nakedness is a sin outside marriage because it reveals something that is to be enjoyed only between a married couple. The reason Noah cursed his son, Ham, was because Ham saw his father's nakedness. The other two sons went to great effort to keep from seeing their father's nakedness. For this, they were blessed. As Christians, we will be judged for our part in displaying our nudity and for viewing the nudity of others. When we say judged, we know that God looks at the intent of the heart. We all know that there are times we may view someone's body with a pure intent, such as changing a baby's diaper,

22

dressing children, or taking care of someone's medical needs.

However, primarily when it comes to the subject of nudity, it is only to be enjoyed between husband and wife. Our bodies and nakedness are how we enjoy that experience together. When we look at Leviticus 18:6-18, we read:

None of you shall approach to any that is near of kin to him, to uncover *their* nakedness: I am the LORD. The nakedness of thy father, or the nakedness of thy mother, shalt thou not uncover: she *is* thy mother; thou shalt not uncover her nakedness. The nakedness of thy father's wife shalt thou not uncover: it *is* thy father's nakedness. The nakedness of thy sister, the daughter of thy father, or daughter of thy mother, *whether she be* born at home, or born abroad, *even* their nakedness thou shalt not uncover. The nakedness of thy son's daughter, or of thy daughter's daughter, even their nakedness thou shalt not uncover: for theirs is thine own nakedness. The nakedness of thy father's wife's daughter, begotten of thy father, she *is* thy sister, thou shalt not uncover her nakedness. Thou shalt not uncover the nakedness of thy father's sister: she *is* thy father's near kinswoman. Thou shalt not uncover the nakedness of thy mother's sister: for she is thy mother's near kins-woman. Thou shalt not uncover the nakedness of thy father's brother, thou shalt not approach to his wife: she *is* thine aunt. Thou shalt not uncover the nakedness of thy daughter in law: she *is* thy son's wife; thou shalt not uncover her nakedness. Thou shalt not uncover the nakedness of thy brother's wife: it is thy brother's nakedness. Thou shalt not uncover the nakedness of a woman and her daughter, neither shalt thou take her son's daughter, or her daughter's daughter, to uncover her nakedness; for they *are* her near kinswomen: it is wickedness. Neither shalt thou take a wife to her sister, to vex her, to uncover her nakedness, beside the other in her life time.

This passage makes it very clear that to reveal our nakedness, or to seek to uncover someone else's body, is sinful. And yet, some try to argue that this is an Old Testament principle and not meant for us today. This, however, was not ceremonial law, but moral law. Just like any Old Testament command, if its principle is backed up in the New Testament, it is still very much applicable. (See Matthew 5:28.) The word that is used commonly throughout Leviticus 18 is "uncover," which means there should be coverings that conceal intimate body areas.

This text also speaks of the sin of incest. In those days, incest was a problem and this violation is still prevalent today. Statistics tell us that now, in the twenty-first century, one out of three girls is violated sexually, and surprisingly, it is often someone close to the family who commits the violation. Relationships should not be blended in such a way that could lead to perversion. Christian counselors agree that a sure way for that to happen is to allow young, immodestly dressed girls to be in the company of older men.

The Draw of Sin

The third reason nakedness outside of marriage is sinful is because of the draw sex has upon humanity. Men are sexually attracted to women in a greater degree than women to men. Nothing gets a man's attention quicker than a beautiful and attractive lady who is flaunting her body with clothing that accentuates what she looks like naked. Although ladies are also sexual creatures, their vices are more of the attention, affirmation, and feelings of love that sex brings to them.

When a man is tempted, as described in Proverbs 7, and he gives his attention to the wayward woman, a positive and negative force is created. These two forces feed off one another, drawing the man and woman together.

With that being said, no one spiritually minded can justify adultery. One of the Ten Commandments is, "Thou shalt not commit adultery" (Exodus 20:14). The Bible also states, "Thou shalt not covet thy neighbour's house, thou shalt not covet thy neighbour's wife, nor his manservant, nor his maidservant, nor his ox, nor his ass, nor any thing that *is* thy neighbour's" (Exodus 20:17). As God's people, we are commanded not to lust after and/or be desirous of another man's wife. Why? For the simple biblical fact that her beauty is to be enjoyed by her husband only.

Jesus said in Matthew 5:28, "But I say unto you, That whosoever looketh on a woman to lust after her hath committed adultery with her already in his heart." Yes, Jesus said that even looking at a woman lustfully is committing adultery in your heart. The same is true of women who look lustfully at a man. Regardless of gender, adultery begins in the heart.

Even though the person lusting is the one that sins, if you cause someone to sin, you are an accessory to their sin. Notice two small words in the verse about committing adultery in the heart. Jesus said that man had already committed adultery "with her." In Romans 14:13 it says, "Let us not therefore judge one another any more: but judge this rather, that no man put a stumbling block or an occasion to fall in *his* brother's way."

Now ladies, before you write me off, I will discuss the man's responsibility, so bear with me for a little bit. Please take some time to think about the many men in the Bible, such as David, Samson,

Solomon, and King Herod, who fell into sin. Many of their sinful actions can be traced to a woman and the draw of her sexuality. Do you think those ladies were faultless?

Distinction is the Goal

I think we would agree that nakedness is sinful, but what else does the Bible teach about our exterior appearance, and how we specifically cover ourselves? The Bible is very clear that men and women are different creatures. Genesis 1:27 states, "So God created man in his *own* image, in the image of God created he him; male and female created he them."

While the gender of some animals are easily detected, like a hen and a rooster, in other animals, like snakes, it is very hard to tell the difference. The differences between men and women, however, are evident. Externally, women have different facial features, facial hair, build, hips, and many other areas than those of their male counterparts. Internally, God gives women different hormones and physical structure than men.

Likewise, I truly believe that God wants ladies' outward adornment to be different than men's. Look at Deuteronomy 22:5: "The woman shall not wear that which pertaineth unto a man, neither shall a man put on a woman's garment: for all that do so *are* abomination unto the LORD thy God." God is very clear that among His people a woman should not dress to look like a man, nor a man to look like a woman.

Now, I must go up a side stream a little while, but promise to come back quickly. I have never bought into the notion that this verse says that a lady wearing pants is an abomination to God. We will deal with the pants issue later, but this is a far stretch for this verse.

I understand why well-meaning pastors and Christians use this verse to support such a theory. It is easy to come up with the wrong conclusion if you believe pants are only for men.

When used in such a manner, someone can stand behind the Bible and argue, "You might not like what I say, but that is what Scripture teaches." Though this is convenient, it is not being honest with the Word of God.

There was a time when I read this verse and tried to convince myself that a woman wearing pants was sinful. However, I never could agree with that logic from this verse. After all, culottes are pants, and pastors and Christians who take the stand of absolutely no pants often approve wholeheartedly of culottes. I struggled with the modesty issue, the distinction of pants, and if they are only men's items of attire. This has been one of the motives for us to write this book—to sort out our thoughts about what the Bible says on this issue.

This verse is speaking of distinction between the genders. If pants are not distinct, then I would have to conclude that culottes are not distinct either. Culottes are modest, legged, loose pants that appear as skirts from a distance.

I must direct you to the history of culottes. Wikipedia states:

> The word *culottes* is of French language origin. Historically, the word 'culottes' has always referred to the knee-breeches commonly worn by gentlemen of the European upper-classes from the late Middle Ages or Renaissance through the early 19th century. Culottes were normally closed and fastened about the leg, to the knee, by either buttons, a strap and buckle, or by a draw-string.[3]

From my study, I have determined that culottes were very loose and were fastened at the knees. The Wikipedia article goes on to say:

> Another latter-day use of the word **culottes** describes a split or divided skirt. During the Victorian Era (mid-to-late-nineteenth century), long split skirts were developed for horseback riding so that women could sit astride a man's saddle rather than riding side-saddle. The term 'culottes' was co-opted from the original French definition of the word to describe these split riding skirts. Later, split skirts were developed to

provide women more freedom to do activities such as gardening, cleaning, bike riding, etc. and still look like one is wearing a skirt. [4]

Now why would I add this? I want to go back to the argument that if you say that pants are men's attire, then likewise culottes are too. They started out like pants and evolved from loose pants to a skirt-like pant. From the prior argument, this would have made them of men's origin; thus being a man's attire.

However, just like most people would not automatically associate pants as only men's attire today, they would not know that culottes were of men's origin unless it was presented to them, or they personally had studied the matter as I have done.

I must also direct you to Deuteronomy 22:11, which is in the same context and sheds some light on the chapter's meaning. It states, "Thou shalt not wear a garment of divers sorts, *as* of woollen and linen together." God did not want His people wearing garments that were of mixed fibers. This practice was a part of pagan worship in those days. God didn't want His people to associate with people of paganism. Similarly, He does not want His people to dress opposite of their gender.

Just as God wanted His people to be distinct and separated from the pagan cultures back then, He still desires His children to be separate from the very same today. I want to deal with a subject a little later concerning the new contemporary Christian culture, in which many have taken on the appearance of the pagan culture and the Babylonian garments of the world. When you look at these so-called Christian rock bands, they look like and sound like the bands that worship Satan. (These are the same bands that I personally listened to and worshipped before I was saved!) There is little to no distinction. I believe this is contrary to biblical principles.

So, before we move back to the point of discerning the distinction of men's or women's attire, I want to let my readers know that I have read books from popular Independent Baptist sources, though I will not purposely mention or quote them. Unfortunately, some of these well-known preachers and authors do more to hurt this particular issue than help it. They translate from the Hebrew and Greek, playing with words. I checked the Greek and Hebrew definitions that they use, and found that these authors add many of their own words to make their definitions say what they want them to say. I truly believe that there are enough biblical principles to make a firm stand concerning Christian dress without manipulating the Bible.

The whole issue of pants rose out of distaste and disgust for the world and its fashions. (And that is fine.) I can fully understand why many men who have pastored thirty years or so, especially during the time when the norm was that all the ladies wore dresses and skirts, stood fast when culture changed, and set about to justify their stand. They looked to Scripture to affix their conviction, as illustrated in Proverbs 24:21, "My son, fear thou the LORD and the king: *and* meddle not with them that are given to change." However, these well-meaning pastors, and even godly pastors trying to do right, have not been honest with the Scripture in some points. Many pastors may not like the fact that culture has changed, but we must deal with the issue biblically and not from a cultural standpoint. Just like the opening illustration with the missionary and the culture that said women didn't have to wear tops because it was hot and easier to nurse the young, we would expect that when the culture is faced with what God says, they would obey the Scripture, and not their culture.

Similarly, if the Bible does not say something is sin, then we cannot make it so, no matter how much we hate the cultural change. We can promote that some attire may be *best*, and set the standard for the church because God has given pastors that right. (This issue will be dealt with more later.)

Now, let's come back. God wants men and women to be distinctly different and requires this of them pertaining to their body and clothes/coverings. God says that to be a cross-dresser is an abomination to Him. Let's look at 1 Corinthians 11:14-15: "Doth not even nature itself teach you, that, if a man have long hair, it is a shame unto him? But if a woman have long hair, it is a glory to her: for her hair is given her for a covering." Again, God, by design, made men and women different, and this distinction needs to be kept intact.

Here is an old quote detailing the distinction:

The dress of females differed from that of males less than is customary among us. Yet there was a distinction; and Moses expressly forbade any exchange of apparel between the sexes, Deuteronomy 22:5, a custom associated with immodesty, and with the worship of certain idols. It is not clear for what reason clothing in which linen and wollen were woven together was prohibited, Deuteronomy 22:11; but probably it had reference to some superstitious usage of heathenism. In Isaiah 3:16-23, mention is made of the decorations common among the Hebrew women of that day; among which seem to be included tunics, embroidered vests, wide flowing mantles, girdles, veils, caps of network, and metallic ornaments for the ears and nose, for the neck, arms, fingers, and ankles; also smelling-bottles and metallic mirrors. . . [5]

Purposeful in Our Dress

God also wants us to be purposeful in the way we dress. In 1 Timothy 2:9-10, it says, "In like manner also, that women adorn themselves in modest apparel, with shamefacedness and sobriety; not with broided hair, or gold, or pearls, or costly array; But (which becometh women professing godliness) with good works."

God desires that ladies wear on the outside that which represents them on the inside. Jesus said to the Pharisees, "Woe unto you, scribes and Pharisees, hypocrites! for ye make clean the outside of the cup and of the platter, but within they are full of extortion and excess. Thou blind Pharisee, cleanse first that which is within the cup and platter, that the outside of them may be clean also" (Matthew 23:25-26).

God makes it clear that we should not appear one way on the outside, yet be different on the inside. There are a couple of different applications from this verse. We can appear beautiful outside, however, be corrupt on the inside. The order, however, should be from the inside out. When we get the inside right, the outside appearance should follow suit.

In some good, fundamental churches, emphasis is put on the exterior appearance; however, the heart attitude is not addressed. Often children who grow up in these kinds of churches and Christian schools think that by dressing right, they can meet others' expectations of living for the Lord. It is often easy to conform to standards, but, as Christians, we are to be transformed from the inside out. Romans 12:2 states, "And be not conformed to this world: but be ye transformed by the renewing of your mind, that ye may prove what *is* that good, and acceptable, and perfect, will of God." The exterior never produces righteousness. I have found that rules without a relationship breeds rebellion. This is the reason we are concerned with the way we present ourselves; it is because of our relationship with the Lord. This really goes to the heart of the matter concerning modesty. We are modest because of who we are in Christ.

As we look at the verses in I Timothy, there are many things that I think are indictments against us as Christians. Often we will preach about modesty, but this subject is not only about whether a lady wears a pair of blue jeans, a miniskirt, culottes, shorts, or any other fad that may pop up in the future. The context of the passage is speaking of the woman's motive for wearing her jewelry, the way she does her hair, and how her display draws attention to her outward appearance rather than her heart attitude. In truth, her motive represents her heart.

I can tell you that often our churches are full of women with brightly painted fingernails, fancy dresses, and flashy jewelry. If their only motive is to draw attention to themselves, they need to examine their heart motive for the way they have adorned themselves. Some of these adornments can be as bad as wearing seductive attire to church. Dressing up is not a negative thing and a woman does not have to look like an old maid to be godly. However, our outward appearance is a matter of the heart.

The word *modesty* is an interesting word. It speaks of being orderly, i.e., decorous, of good behavior. Basically, all our exterior clothing and adornment should purposely represent who we are in Christ. Just like the harlot dressed with purpose to lure men, Christian women and men are to dress with purpose in contrast to the world. Our purpose should be to avoid making someone lust or stumble. And, our purpose should be to invite the lost and dying world to a relationship with our Heavenly Father. Modesty in appearance, rather than nudity, can accomplish these purposes.

There is also another charge that one must consider, and that is the area of weight. The definition of modesty just explained above would thus conclude that being overweight is not a good testimony of our bodies. It shows lack of control.

I realize that some people may have medical conditions, such as thyroid problems or other serious issues. On the other hand, weight is often a cultural problem that we struggle with because of sedentary lifestyles or over-indulgence in fattening foods.

Modesty also means that we present ourselves in a neat and clean fashion. There is an epidemic of casual Christianity today with people showing up for church services in shorts, sandals, and novelty T-shirts. There is little to no respect for themselves, their testimonies, or God's house.

Before I became a Christian, I had long hair and played in rock bands. I was intimidated by Christians and how they dressed up. When I appeared at a church dressed with my Metallica T-shirt and biker boots, I was surprised at my own reaction to the people's dress.

I was not surprised that everyone was dressed up. I had anticipated that. But with soft, God-honoring hymns in the background, I remember thinking to myself, "These people care enough about what they are doing to dress up for it, almost like they are going to see the President every Sunday!" Now, in hindsight, I know they were dressing up for Someone special—the King of Kings and Lord of Lords. Therefore, part of modesty is the idea of giving our best within biblical principles without being flashy about it.

Now let me go back to the progressive Christian culture. Today, well-meaning Christians have taken on the worldview that we must be like the world to win them. You don't find that in the Scriptures. In fact, what you find is just the opposite. Anyone who diligently and honestly studies the Scriptures will come to the same conclusion. Some use Paul's testimony, "I am made all things to all *men*" (1 Corinthians 9:22b), to support their view of becoming of the world to win the world. Paul did not mean he took on their manner of appearance, but that he spoke to them in a way they could understand in order to reach them with the Gospel. Always remember that the Bible never contradicts itself. Paul would not tell us to do something that would contradict the scriptural principles of distinction and separation.

The new Christian contemporary culture follows the world in many of the areas of exterior adornment. These Christians may say that they wholeheartedly believe in God's will; however, as Jesus told the Pharisees, "Thou blind Pharisee, cleanse first that which is within the cup and platter, that the <u>outside of them may be clean also</u>" (Matthew 23:26; emphasis added). God is concerned about both the inside and outside of the cup (bodies).

Are Pants Men's Attire?

I promised we'd come back to the issue of women wearing pants. Many of those who dictate that pants are sinful and an abomination to God use the text from I Timothy chapter two. The Greek word *katastole* is used in the original text. This word is generally translated into English as the word *apparel*. Some people, however, take the Greek root words *kata* and *stole* and try to limit the definition of the combined word to mean the text is only speaking of a *dress* only. I disagree with the quoted text below. I am purposely not acknowledging the author because I don't wish to bash anyone, only expose how the person came to the wrong conclusion.

> 'Apparel' today is a very general term that means 'any article of clothing.' But did you know that in 1611 the word 'apparel' meant 'loose, long flowing garment?' Look it up in an old Oxford English Dictionary that has the archaic meanings of words. Furthermore, the Greek word is *katastole* which is an EXACTING WORD, and it is the ONLY place in the Bible where it is used. There are lots of words for clothing, attire, etc., but this word comes from a verb form which means 'to lower.' It denoted a loose-fitting outer garment, which was LONG. Paul used this word specifically to tell women that they are to wear long DRESSES. Pants, miniskirts, tight dresses, etc. cannot fit the definition of this exacting word. Consult your Vine's Dictionary for verification of this word definition. [6]

I could spend a lot of time here and debate words, definitions, and root word usage. There are some giant leaps of logical thought within that quote. Look at it again and judge for yourself.

I don't believe the author is being honest with the Scripture or the Greek language. The Greek word *katastole* is formed by two other Greek words, *kata* and *stole*. That I agree with, but the Greek word for *katastole*, is defined by *Thayer's Greek-English Lexicon* "a lowering, letting down a garment, let down dress, attire." You will find this consistent with all the other Greek Lexicons. For example, *Vine's Expository Dictionary* says, "was primarily a garment let down; hence, dress, attire."[7]

How does one make the leap from those definitions to "Paul used this word specifically to tell women that they are to wear long DRESSES"? Remember at this time, there were no dresses, but tunics, which men wore too.

The word *dress*, therefore, would be a general word not speaking of specific clothing, but a general description of all attire. For example, "They were dressed for success." However, even from the author's own definition, pants, if they are long and loose, could fit within these perimeters. Again as we have seen throughout the Word of God on this subject, God only says that clothing must be distinct, modest (not revealing/orderly), and different from the world. There is nothing new that can be gleaned from the Greek here, other than what is on the surface. We must be careful not to construe biblical messages with our own definitions of these Greek words, and not be like some who have added to Scripture by adding to the translated words and definitions, then applying their new term or terms to God's Word and calling their interpretation biblical.

The outward adornment we choose should purposely represent us inwardly as Christians. This is contrary to popular belief that we should conform to the pagan and sinful world that we live in, a world that worships sex and sensual music. When Peter addressed wives in 1 Peter 3:3-4 he said, "Whose adorning let it not be that outward adorning of plaiting the hair, and of wearing of gold, or of putting on of apparel; But let it be the hidden man of the heart, in that which is not corruptible, even the ornament of a meek and quiet spirit, which is in the sight of God of great price."

How Do I Judge What is Right and Wrong?

With all these things said, let's go full force into the how-to area of choosing what is right and wrong when it comes to dress. Again, we must base our conclusions on God's principles and the culture that surrounds us.

Does My Dress Cover the Intimate Parts of My Body?

There is a great debate about the subject of modesty. For some people, modesty is found in a string bikini that has less cotton than an aspirin bottle. Others consider anything not plain-looking in appearance immodest.

In contemplating what constitutes modesty of dress, we can rely a little on the precedent from biblical culture, where women dressed in a way that clearly covers their bottoms, breasts, bellies, etc., because these are the areas that are for intimacy—that are to be enjoyed by married couples.

Let's take a look again at Adam and Eve in Genesis 3:7, "And the eyes of them both were opened, and they knew that they were naked; and they sewed fig leaves together, and made themselves aprons."

The coverings they made for themselves are interesting. They sewed leaves together to cover many parts of their bodies. Some of the unbiblical pictures we see with Adam and Eve with just a leaf over their private parts are not accurate. The word "apron" is used, which was probably different than what we think of finding in a kitchen today. They made these in an attempt to cover their nakedness and were probably similar to a blacksmith's apron worn to protect him from fire. Most likely, the aprons were a full covering.

But, notice that God was not convinced these coverings were adequate. Genesis 3:21 says, "Unto Adam also and to his wife did the LORD God make coats of skins, and clothed them." The word *coats* is indicative of robes, and because God made them, He would have followed His later commands about distinction of clothing between men and women. I am convinced that Adam's coat was recognizably different from Eve's.

Again, referring back to Nancy Leigh DeMoss' booklet, *The Look: Does God Really Care What I Wear?* she states, "by contrast the 'garments' that God made for Adam and Eve (Genesis 3:21) were 'tunics' or 'coats.' Various Bible dictionaries agree that this term refers to an article of clothing that covers the body at least from the neck to the knees." [8]

So, the attire would have been long, loose, and concealing. We see this born out in the fact that up until modern Western culture took over, many men and women wore tunics. Traditionally, men's tunics were different from women's in that a man's tunic was designed for work or battle while a woman's tunic was made for ease in maneuvering around the home and taking care of children. From my studies, I found that a man's tunic has traditionally been shorter than a woman's, allowing him more agility in fighting and defending his home.

Maybe you ask, "Well, why don't we wear tunics today, since that is what we see in the Bible?" Some people in the Middle East do still wear tunics. But, the majority of my readers don't live there. Much of the style of dress and reasoning behind the tunics has to do with climate. There has also been a change in culture and men wearing tunics might give the appearance of a man wearing a dress. Here we are back again at the command for the genders to be distinct from one another.

One time, during my unsaved days, I was at a hippie commune. I saw a tall person with long hair who was wearing a dress. (It was actually a tunic/robe.) I thought it was a woman, and was surprised when I discovered it was a man!

Do you remember what I said about culture affecting how we dress? We don't live in the Middle East, but we live in Western culture. We must choose to wear clothing that does not reveal our nudity, is gender distinct, reflects Christ, and doesn't make us look like weirdos. Yes, we wear much of what the world does within our own customs and culture, but must do so while still applying God's commands for modesty.

Those who want to take dress to the extreme and make it a letter of the law on how ladies should dress need to be careful. They can easily paint themselves into a corner, because honestly, the majority of the garments you find in the Bible are robes and tunics. I don't know about you, but that attire is not on my agenda to wear.

I have known some men who play the bagpipes and wear kilts, and though kilts may have a Scottish heritage, they still look like miniskirts on men. I would not personally wear them because they are not distinct in appearance.

So the grand question is how close does your dress come to biblical principles and still fit within Western culture? I truly believe that any clothing that shows off the size, form, or the cleavage of the breast is not modest. I am fully aware that there are many women who are large breasted and have difficulty finding shirts that are not snug in the chest area. Also, God obviously made women different from men, including the shape of their breasts. I am not suggesting buying shirts three times the size; however, shirts, blouses, and sweaters should fit in such a way that there's room to breathe!

When it comes to the pelvic area, thighs, and the bottom, the clothing should not accentuate nor reveal the inner thigh and the shape and form of the bottom. A modest approach does not reveal these private and intimate areas. I will talk about this in more detail in the section concerning men's temptations. Your clothing should not draw attention to your body, but to your godliness.

Dresses and skirts are usually a safe bet when it comes to making sure that a lady's clothing is not showing her nudity. If they are long, don't show cleavage, and not form fitting, there is little question about it.

Is My Dress Distinct from Men's Clothing?

Some women contend that this whole dress issue is unfair to them, and people are trying to put them in bondage by dictating that they look like a "plain Jane." I understand their thinking, but it is not true. Women can make their clothes distinct in appearance and style, and still be beautifully modest, fitting in with biblical principles. I believe that during Bible times women did this with their robes and tunics. They can still do that today.

Now here come the questions that many have been waiting for. "Are pants men's attire? Is it okay for ladies to wear pants?" Honestly and biblically, pants are not designated for either gender. Breeches were worn as undergarments, and in the Bible we only see them worn by priests. Exodus 28:42 states, "And thou shalt make them linen breeches to cover their nakedness; from the loins even unto the thighs they shall reach."

Pants were made to cover the priest's nakedness, and one could easily argue that nowhere can we find ordinary men choosing to wear them. There is no command, law, or even custom that dictated regular men to wear them.

A good argument for wearing pants is that in striving to be modest, pants worn under robes would provide a better form of modesty. Don't forget, however, that they were like underwear and really were not intended to be outer clothing.

Can I say that pants on ladies are sinful? No! But, I can say, in my opinion, they are not what is best *at times*. I can also state, that many of the pants that are on the market, the clothing racks, and many Christian bodies are not modest. Most designers have no interest in making them so. Therefore, if a lady chooses to wear pants, she will have to be very selective. If a lady chooses to take the high road (which is always the best path in the Christian life), and wears a dress, then there is no chance of her being mistakenly identified as a man, for men do not wear dresses in our culture.

So, if a lady wears a pair of pants, is she an abomination to God? No. I've heard many arguments that pants are only for men because they were originally created for men, not for women. True, history does show that men have traditionally worn pants. We still see this today when we walk towards a public bathroom. The pictures show a woman in a dress and a man in pants. Likewise, do you ever wonder why girls' bikes are different then boys'? Girls' bikes have a dip in the frame so ladies in skirts and dresses can ride them in a modest fashion.

However, you would be hard pressed to prove the original intent of the invention of pants. As we mentioned, pants probably started out as underwear. I would guess that over the course of time they evolved into what we have today.

Throughout history, we have seen the use of pants more as a man's attire than a woman's. But, in today's culture and our modern times, that is no longer the case. If I see someone in slacks, I do not automatically assume it is a man. As early as fifty years ago, a person might have been confused, but not today. (And while some might read this and say, "God is the same yesterday, today and forever," you only find breeches in the Scriptures as being an article of clothing for the priests. So, if

that is your argument, take off your pants, get a
tunic, and put breeches underneath!) Culture has
changed and will continue to change, just as it has
done since man first hung his tunic on a coat rack.

Some will go on to say that there is little
distinction between men's and women's pants, that
these are essentially unisex and therefore do not
provide adequate separation/distinction of the
genders. Well, again, I must go back to the tunics.
One does not see that much distinction between
them either. Though I believe there were differences in color, pattern, etc.

I find there is also that kind of distinction with
some slacks, especially with the polyester slacks
worn by some of the older ladies. There are many
different styles of pants that are distinctly ladylike,
feminine, and yet are still modest apparel.

You could make the same argument concerning
the unisex designs for button up or collared shirts,
saying that women's and men's designs are not
distinct. They look the same from a distance but
upon closer inspection, they button from the
opposite side. Can you recognize from a distance
which side of the shirt the buttons are on? I didn't
think so. The distinction comes from the colors,
design, and modesty factor.

Zodervan's Pictorial Dictionary states, "A few
articles of female clothing carried somewhat the
same name and same basic pattern as a man's, yet
there was always sufficient difference . . . so that in

appearance, the line of demarcation between men and women could readily be detected."[9]

As I write this, it may sound like I am arguing that it is okay for women to wear pants. However, that is not what I am doing. I am presenting all the arguments so you can decide for yourself. For me personally, there is nothing I find more ladylike, modest, and more easily distinguishable between the genders than a dress/skirt.

Ladies who wear form-fitting slacks that reveal their bottoms or their figure are not practicing modesty. In my opinion, they reveal too much of their body. Should they choose to wear pants or capris they should be loose enough that they don't form to the shape of the body.

I realize it is difficult for ladies to find appropriate pants today. As we stated, manu-facturers and designers are not striving to make clothes that are modest. Instead, they want women to show off their figures. And they are ever changing the look so that women will buy more clothing. When women wear immodest clothing, it reminds me of a saying I heard once, "If it's not for sale, take the sign out of the window!" You must make sure that you're not displaying to others the goods God gave you for your husband. I have noticed that when ladies are confronted with having to wear loose pants, some say, "What is the use then?" This attitude reveals their motives for wearing the tight-fitting pants. Remember, Chris-tian modesty is a matter of the heart.

Isaiah 47:1-3 sheds some light on the subject:

Come down, and sit in the dust, O virgin daughter of Babylon, sit on the ground: *there is* no throne, O daughter of the Chaldeans: for thou shalt no more be called tender and delicate. Take the millstones, and grind meal: uncover thy locks, make bare the leg, uncover the thigh, pass over the rivers. Thy nakedness shall be uncovered, yea, thy shame shall be seen: I will take vengeance, and I will not meet *thee as* a man.

God makes it clear that there is shame associated with "make bare the leg, uncover the thigh."

As I write this, I need to restate part of my motive. It is to bring to the surface that a dogmatic stance on the issue of women wearing pants, calling it sin and an abomination to the Lord, is not supported by Scripture. I truly believe the subject of women wearing pants comes down to personal preference, personal liberty, and personal situations. However, if a lady chooses to wear pants, she should do so with all modesty and be careful that the pants are loose enough so as not to reveal the shape of her pelvic, bottom, or thighs. A lady could also wear a long shirt/blouse that would cover up her bottom and maintain a more modest approach, if she chooses to wear pants.

An example of where pants may be deemed appropriate for ladies would be in the Northern or colder climates. In such areas, snow pants are often worn for recreation. They are big, puffy, loose, and do not form to the body. Snow pants are quite useful when shoveling or playing in the snow. I don't see anything immodest about this type of pant. There is an occasion for it. I also know of many older ladies (and some younger) in the North who wear loose-fitting slacks during the winter because their blood is very thin and they are cold most of the time. These women wear pants in order to stay warm enough to keep from getting ill. Another example can be found in mountain regions or for horseback riding. Naturally, you want to protect your legs in a mountainous area, or from the coarse hair on the horse. Again, there are pants on the market that are not low-ride hip huggers. A woman can wear loose jeans, sweat pants, or athletic pants that will serve the purpose of the circumstances or event and still maintain a decorum of modesty. With this freedom of personal preference, liberty, and situation, one must not brag about that freedom to another who may not have the same personal convictions of choice. If you know there are people in your life who do not hold to the same convictions as you, keep your freedom to yourself. You're not being a hypocrite; you are abstaining from judging them and their convictions.

Paul states in Romans 14:1-4:

> Him that is weak in the faith receive ye, *but* not to doubtful disputations. For one believeth that he may eat all things: another, who is weak, eateth herbs. Let not him that eateth despise him that eateth not; and let not him which eateth not judge him that eateth: for God hath received him. Who art thou that judgest another man's servant? to his own master he standeth or falleth. Yea, he shall be holden up: for God is able to make him stand.

Now I know that it is talking about food in the context, but just a little later the Bible brings in a broader scope.

> Let us not therefore judge one another any more: but judge this rather, that no man put a stumbling block or an occasion to fall in *his* brother's way. I know, and am persuaded by the Lord Jesus, that *there is* nothing unclean of itself: but to him that esteemeth any thing to be unclean, to him *it is* unclean. But if thy brother be grieved with *thy* meat, now walkest thou not charitably. Destroy not him with thy meat, for whom Christ died. (Romans 14:13-15).

As Christians, we are not to cause someone to stumble because of our liberty. I know that this can be tricky because with our choice of clothing, we are displaying our convictions and our freedoms.

The book of Romans goes on to say, "It is good neither to eat flesh, nor to drink wine, nor any thing whereby thy brother stumbleth, or is offended, or is made weak" (Romans 14:21). If a woman knows of someone who is genuinely offended by women in pants, or any other article of clothing, to the point that it becomes a stumbling block to the other person, the offending person is biblically commanded to refrain from wearing that item around the one who would be offended. I don't wear a tie when I go door-to-door soul winning. I have found that many people associate the suit and tie with other religious groups who have offended them. They are then reluctant to open their doors. For them, the wearing or not wearing of a tie might not be a personal conviction, but I want nothing of my outward appearance to offend them and hinder the Gospel.

Romans 14:22-23 really sums up the issue, "Hast thou faith? have it to thyself before God. Happy *is* he that condemneth not himself in that thing which he alloweth. And he that doubteth is damned if he eat, because *he eateth* not of faith: for whatsoever is not of faith is sin." If you have a conviction about pants, don't wear them. If you don't have a conviction about wearing pants, don't flaunt the fact that you have no problem in front of them that may have a different conviction. Now some may say that pants are not modest. There are some pants that are not modest, just as there are dresses and skirts that are inappropriate. But, it is less likely that a man will be visually and sexually aroused by a woman in loose pants than in form-fitting ones.

What about dresses and skirts? I have heard ladies argue that some dresses are not modest. May I say thank you for stating the obvious, but the immodesty of some skirts and dresses does not justify you wearing pants that are not modest either. Two wrongs don't make a right.

There are dresses that are patterned after the world by being flashy and revealing and they are sinful. Women in skirts, even skirts that come past the knee when sitting, can be very suggestive, arousing men when the woman crosses her legs. One must choose appropriate dresses, skirts, blouses, and pants that are not immodest. Again, I challenge the ladies to find any attire that is more biblically distinctive or modest than a chaste dress or skirt. Needless to say, miniskirts and the like are always immodest.

I can already hear the ladies crying foul. Is it my job to eliminate a brother from sinning? Let me say that you and I both have a biblical responsibility not to be a stumbling block to anyone. Romans 14 instructs us that we are to go out of our way and, at times, surrender our liberty so as not to be a stumbling block to our brothers and sisters in Christ.

Do you remember Cain's response when God questioned him about his brother? "And the LORD said unto Cain, Where is Abel thy brother? And he said, I know not: *Am* I my brother's keeper?" (Genesis 4:9). Cain was cursed because he murdered his brother. When God cursed Cain, He was telling him, "Yes, you are your brother's keeper." Likewise, we also are our brothers' and sisters' keeper and we are to support them in their walk with Christ, not lead them to sin. "For none of us liveth to himself, and no man dieth to himself" (Romans 14:7).

As we already mentioned, men are sexual creatures. They are turned on by sight, whereas ladies are usually turned on by emotions. There are ladies who crave attention that comes from people looking at them, thinking they look attractive, thus they dress in a way to get that attention. They may get their attention, but at the same time, they lead a man to sin in his mind and heart. Regarding attention among females, how many ladies do you hear complimenting each other about how good the other looks? It is almost like a girl's handshake. Often when a lady gives a compliment, she wants and expects one in return.

So the question one must ask when choosing attire, including dress, makeup, etc. is, "What is my motive and what reactions can I expect to my exterior adornment?" You must choose your dress with purpose. When you see the big picture, as

God does, you will want to do this. Many of you ladies already do this but may not realize it.

Let me give you another example. I call this a child molester test. Let's say you have a teenage daughter and a seven-year-old daughter, and you know you are going to be in a room with your girls and ten convicted child molesters. (I know you're saying, "I would never," but we are saying that you do not have a choice.) Before you go into the room, how would you instruct your daughters to dress? I believe you would dress them in a way that would not make them stand out sexually, and perhaps go to extremes to make them not stand out at all. Also, you would make sure they were dressed for safety. When it comes to child molesters, dresses on little girls can make them easy prey, especially short dresses and skirts. Long dresses make it harder, but if you ask my wife, she'd put a pair of loose-fitting overalls on the little seven-year-old girl, just to be on the safe side.

Would you agree that you would be over-protective and dress your daughters as non-seductive as possible? You may think that my analogy is an extreme illustration and does not represent reality. However, let me remind you of the statistics that tell us that one out of three girls is violated sexually, and surprisingly, it is often a family member or someone close to the family who commits the violation. There are sexual predators abundant in our society. Men are bombarded by Satan all day long through billboards, commercials, immodestly dressed women, the Internet, and so on. How sad it is when a man comes to church seeking healing for his soul and a lady's dress, or the lack thereof, continues the temptation. As you can see, there are other things to consider beyond your feelings, attitude, and convictions about the matter.

If you would dress your daughters different so as not to attract men to them, then you must conclude that you should dress different also so as not to lead men to you. If certain clothing can lead men to your daughters, then it can lead men to you also, if not physically, then mentally, which Jesus states is sin.

What Do Your Clothes Say About You?

When we go back to I Timothy chapter 2, the ladies are instructed to dress modest and not bring attention to themselves by their outward appearance, but to their godliness of the heart. Again, there is a purpose for what we wear for all occasions.

Billions of dollars are spent every year on uniforms. Wal-Mart has them, restaurants, stores, and just about every business that wants to portray an image. Some businesses, like the restaurant Hooters, use the way they have their waitresses dress to lure men in to drink and buy food. Christians are on the job 24/7 and should always be representing Christ. God is very concerned about the exterior. He gives many commands about how we are to present our outward bodies. He tells the priests what to wear, the ladies to dress modestly, and men what to wear in battle, etc.

If you walk down the street and see a man in a blue uniform with a badge, what would you think his occupation was? You probably answered, "A police officer." Yes, because of the way he was dressed. A lot of stores, restaurants, and other establishments will not allow you to come inside unless you have on a shirt and shoes. Or better yet, golfers must wear certain attire while playing in a gated, upscale golf course. Long story short, there are expectations from our world about people's appearance. Those expectations fall upon the godly and ungodly to conform.

Since worldly businesses and establishments set dress codes, why can't there be a precedent set for the house of God and for Christians representing Christ in the world? When walking down the street, let's say you see a lady with a short skirt; thick, flashy makeup; and fishnet stockings. What would be your first impression? Probably a hooker, or an unsaved person, at the least? Your first guess would not be, "I bet she is a missionary sharing the Good News of Christ."

When I was saved, I had very long hair. It was the style in the mid-eighties, with the glam rock bands, big hair, tight leather jeans, and so on. After becoming a Christian, I was on fire for the Lord and my life was dedicated to winning others to Him.

The church that I attended was conservative and very traditional. All the men had military haircuts and dressed very professionally. All but me, that is. This was in Blacksburg, Virginia, home of Virginia Tech with a reputation of being a party town. I went door to door witnessing for God. The Lord used me and I was able to see some people saved.

One day, however, I was speaking to a gentleman from my church about winning others to the Lord. Though no one had ever told me I needed to cut my hair, I knew that I was different and was ready to argue that I was more effective in winning college students to the Lord.

As we talked, he challenged me about my outward appearance. He said, "Jerry, you have a great burden to see people saved, and you are effective in speaking to the down-and-out person and many of the partying college students because at first glance, you look just like them and they find commonality with your exterior, and as you speak to them, you can tell them how God has changed your heart."

Then he asked me the question, "What if you're knocking on doors and come across a family man with some set traditional values. When he opens the door and sees you, he may be scared by your appearance. As you try to tell him that he needs what you have, his natural response would be,

59

'Look at him! Who is he to tell me that I need to change?'" He paused, then continued. "Just think about your appearance, Jerry. It may be limiting your witness."

That illustration stuck in my heart because I did not want to reach only the down-and-outer, but all men. I had to face the fact that I could be used better by having short hair and a more acceptable appearance. I could reach the down-and-outer with short hair, but would be limited when I tried to reach the up-and-outer.

So what is my point? Christians need to dress with a purpose, and that purpose is to be able to reach people for the glory of God, and likewise not be a temptation. Christian women should not bring attention to their figures, but to their Christian character.

Modest, distinct, separated, and purposeful clothing says a lot about you. It states to people that you're different. (See 2 Corinthians 6:17.) It shows that you have respect for yourself and for the temple God gave you. 1 Corinthians 6:19-20 says, "What? know ye not that your body is the temple of the Holy Ghost *which is* in you, which ye have of God, and ye are not your own? For ye are bought with a price: therefore glorify God in your body, and in your spirit, which are God's."

Modesty also shows humility. If God gave you beauty and an attractive body, it is from God, not of yourself. You are not to be ashamed of your body, but neither are you to flaunt it with pride.

The way you dress speaks volumes about your attitude toward God's gift.

While the world says, "If you got it, flaunt it!" God says, "But he giveth more grace. Wherefore he saith, God resisteth the proud, but giveth grace unto the humble" (James 4:6). Do you remember the woman from Proverbs 7 and what her words and clothes said about her? "And, behold, there met him a woman with the attire of an harlot, and subtil of heart. (She is loud and stubborn; her feet abide not in her house.)" (Proverbs 7:10-11). What do your clothes say about you? That you're hip, seductive, proud, or godly?

Because women's dress styles and choices vary quite a bit, ladies need to be careful that they don't judge one another. Some women will be stricter in their modesty, while some will dress appropriately, yet more relaxed in their rules than others. I have heard some women comment on a plainly-dressed woman and say, "If I looked like her, I would cover it up too." Or maybe, "She's just jealous of the way I look and wants me to cover myself up." And, if truth be told, some ladies dress modest not because of being a stumbling block to men but to keep from being embarrassed, especially those with weight issues. It's not about others, but about you, your relationship and responsibility to God, and your responsibility not to be a stumbling block to men.

Ladies, as you consider the form and type of clothes you wear, will people say, "This lady has beauty, there is something different about her, and she is humble"? Will they say that you have an inner glow about you, rather than comment about your outward dress?

What is Appropriate for the Occasion?

I think outward adornment boils down to what is appropriate for the occasion. Just as uniforms communicate a message, so does a Christian's attire. We need to make sure that our outward adornment is modest, distinctive, and separate from the world. At the same time, we must use common sense. For example, even though I am a pastor, if I am going to paint the church, I don't need to wear a suit and a tie. I may not look the way I normally dress, but jeans and an old shirt would be more appropriate. However, I can still maintain a manner of dress befitting a Christian.

As I mentioned earlier, we are Christians 24/7. The way we dress should show that fact. This does not mean, however, that we must wear our Sunday best every place we go. I know some may disagree with that, but I believe as long as my dress does not break scriptural principles and is appropriate, then it's fine.

Let's look at swimming. I know some families that require their young daughters to wear dresses when swimming. Though I respect their convictions, and would not put them down for their decisions, neither would I want them to put me down for not asking my wife to do the same.

I do believe that bikinis and most women's bathing suits are not modest attire when in the presence of someone of the opposite gender other than the woman's husband. And, quite frankly, the designs for many men's bathing suits have become equally inappropriate to wear in front of a woman that is not the man's wife. However, I don't think long, loose shorts and a modest t-shirt on a lady or a man defy the scriptural principles of modesty, separation, or distinction. When dressed with such modesty, you show that that there is something different about you, and that you are being obedient to God.

Yes, some say, "Shorts are just pants with the legs cut short." I could use the same argument that culottes are also pants or argue that dresses when swimming are not modest, for when under the water a dress could be very revealing.

Next, let's talk about what is appropriate attire within the home. At home, we can dress appropriately according to our personal convictions and principles, including shorts, modest pants, etc. Our homes are where we get comfortable and do most of our living. I don't wear a tie or a suit around the house. If company comes over, I may change from my casual clothes and dress a little more professional, but not as though I am in the office. When my wife is cooking and cleaning, with just us and the children at home, she chooses what is comfortable and appropriate for the work she is doing. If she is scrubbing floors, she may wear knee-length shorts or loose-fitting pants. If someone comes over, depending on who it is, she sometimes changes her clothing. You may ask, "Isn't this hypocritical?" I don't believe it is. It is dressing appropriately for the occasion. I liken this example to a dinner party. The invitation might clearly state that the event is "a black-tie affair." Therefore, you would know that you would not be dressed properly if you attended wearing khaki pants and a polo shirt. Someone may argue that they shouldn't have to wear a tie to the party because they don't wear a tie other places. I think the illustration is clear and sheds light on the concept that we do dress differently for different occasions. However, a different dress code for different situations does not make you a hypocrite, but applicable and practical.

Many people believe it is wrong for a church to impose rules of attire for services. I agree that we should not tell someone they cannot come to church unless they wear a dress (ladies) or a tie (men). However, I can't understand why some people have a problem when a church dictates what a person wears if they are in leadership. By leadership, I mean Sunday school teachers, ushers, musicians, etc. I wonder if the people that have a problem with churches saying an usher must wear a tie also have a problem with a store that says no shoes—no service. Probably not.

As a church, and especially when it comes to leadership positions within the church, pastors may want to set guidelines for an image of professionalism. The leadership of the church has the right to do so, just as Wal-Mart, Sears, restaurants, and other places of business have the right to set guidelines for their employees and those who represent their company. As I mentioned earlier, many stores have a dress code for their customers, as well as their employees.

As a pastor, I have a responsibility to take care of my flock. The Bible is clear that church members should follow their pastor's guidelines with a good heart. The author of Hebrews states, "Obey them that have the rule over you, and submit yourselves: for they watch for your souls, as they that must give account, that they may do it with joy, and not with grief: for that *is* unprofitable for you" (Hebrews 13:17).

In the church I pastor, I have set a rule for the women who work in the nursery. The rule states that they wear smocks, similar to hospital nurses' smocks, and that the ladies wear a dress or a knee-length skirt. This prevents their clothing from being soiled when a baby spits up, drools, or vomits. In addition, it tells our visitors that we are professional when taking care of their children. The principle for this rule is no different than what colleges, Christian schools, and other organizations requiring certain dress standards to be adhered to set forth.

You have the freedom of choice to attend or not, but why try to usurp the authority of the leadership, especially when they are not making you sin, but holding you to a higher standard by wearing a dress or modest clothing? Even Burger King and McDonald's demand that children take off their shoes when playing in their indoor playgrounds. As a pastor, I am placed in a position of overseeing all aspects of the ministry. Acts 20:28 says, "Take heed therefore unto yourselves, and to all the flock, over the which the Holy Ghost hath made you overseers. . ."

You may choose your clothing based solely on what is comfortable or convenient. When I choose my clothing and other outer adornments, I go beyond that. I ask myself what is the best attire for the entire ministry? What can best represent the Church and Christ? I do not want to be a stumbling block to visitors, but wish to display profession-alism.

What if pastors and leaders of ministry did not dictate a dress code for workers? What if you walked into your teen girls Sunday school class, and the teacher was wearing a string bikini? Would you say that would be inappropriate? Most would say yes. Why? Because she would be a distraction to the students, the girls would have the wrong example, and the men of the church would be greatly distracted, perhaps sinning in their hearts.

In summary, there is a time and place for most things, even bikinis. I think the appropriate time for such attire would be when a husband and wife are swimming together with no one else around. Also, like with most subjects, you must be guided by the Spirit of God and God's principles. Will there be people that will abuse their liberty? Yes! But, every man and women must give an account of themselves before the Lord.

CHAPTER THREE

To the Ladies (Men's Temptations)

In this chapter, I want to explain a side of the debate that is hard for some ladies to understand. As we have already talked about, many good men in the Bible fell prey to their sexual appetites. Think about what would cause a man who has it all to throw it away for thirty seconds of fame in a strange woman's bed.

Former presidential candidate John Edwards is a perfect example of a man who threw everything he had away because of his temptations. The number of men who have done this is overwhelming. Now I want you to think with me a minute. How many women do you know that have thrown away their careers for a night of sexual escapades? Not very many. They may, over the course of time, be lured by their emotions into a wrong relationship, but not as quickly as a man succumbs to those same temptations.

What is it that makes men so vulnerable? Why is the draw so strong? As stated in chapter one, God wired men and women differently. He did so purposely. God gave woman to man to be a helpmate. Adam did not request it. The Bible tells us, "And the LORD God said, It *is* not good that the man should be alone; I will make him an help meet for him" (Genesis 2:18). Later, in the New Testament, Paul explicitly says that some men need a wife to avoid sexual temptations (ninety-nine percent). "Nevertheless, *to avoid* fornication, let every man have his own wife, and let every woman have her own husband" (1 Corinthians 7:2).

God commanded humanity to replenish the Earth. Scripture states: "And God blessed them, and God said unto them, Be fruitful, and multiply, and replenish the earth, and subdue it: and have dominion over the fish of the sea, and over the fowl of the air, and over every living thing that moveth upon the earth" (Genesis 1:28).

Men and women are to come together in marriage, have a leave and cleave relationship, and replenish the earth. This means we leave all other relationships and are joined together as husband and wife. How does God help this happen? He uses attraction of the two to draw them together. For the woman, God uses a man's affection and attention toward the woman to draw her to him. For the man, God uses a woman's exterior appearance, the man's stimulation through the visual image, and the man's sexual appetite to draw him to her. Thus, you have a magnet-to-metal effect.

A problem for men and women is that God forbids sexual relationships outside the marriage.

Fornication is clearly labeled as sin in the Bible. Christians are to keep their bodies pure, not uniting them with anyone other than a spouse in a sexual way. The results of sexual relations outside a marriage are discussed in 1 Corinthians. "Know ye not that your bodies are the members of Christ? shall I then take the members of Christ, and make *them* the members of an harlot? God forbid. What? know ye not that he which is joined to an harlot is one body? for two, saith he, shall be one flesh" (1 Corinthians 6:15-16). Now let's go to Jesus' words about adultery. "But I say unto you, That whosoever looketh on a woman to lust after her hath committed adultery <u>with her</u> already in his heart" (Matthew 5:28; emphasis added). Please notice the underlined word "<u>with her</u>" that means together. Interesting, don't you think?

So, what is the point? Men can sin in their hearts by being desirous of women sexually. Look at the wording "looketh on a woman to lust." A man may be responding due to the way God has wired men to be visually stimulated, however, his response, instincts, reactions, and thoughts must still be under submission of the Spirit of God.

There are many instances in the Bible that show us that a man's sexual appetite is teased by what he sees. A few of these include:

David (Bathsheba)
Solomon
King Herod (His niece danced before him.)

71

These men were all enticed by what they saw.

I believe that if there is a command in the Bible, it is there because the Lord knew we needed to be instructed how to keep ourselves from naturally doing what is wrong. There is a purpose behind every command. You don't find the command for women not to lust sexually. Though some may, like the harlot in Proverbs chapter 7; raging, sexual desire is usually found in men. In Proverbs 5:18-19, we read, "Let thy fountain be blessed: and rejoice with the wife of thy youth. *Let her be as* the loving hind and pleasant roe; let her breasts satisfy thee at all times; and be thou ravished always with her love" (Proverbs 5:18-19).

God knows Satan can and will use this natural desire within a man, pervert it, and get that man outside of God's will. Just watch ten minutes of television, look at roadside billboards, or surf the Internet. You will see the spiritual fight men face daily.

Statistics show some alarming facts.

1. Fifty-seven percent of pastors say that addiction to pornography is the most sexually damaging issue in their congregations. [10]

2. Ninety percent of children ages eight to sixteen have viewed pornography on the Internet. In most cases, this was done unintentionally. [11]

3. Fifty percent of Promise Keepers' attendees viewed pornography within a week before the event.[12]
4. Twenty-nine percent of born-again adults in the United States feel it is morally acceptable to view movies with explicit sexual behavior. [13]
5. More than seventy percent of men from ages eighteen to thirty-four visit a pornographic site on the Internet in a typical month. [14]
6. Forty-seven percent of families said that pornography was a problem in their home. [15]

Look at Job's statement in the Old Testament: "I made a covenant with mine eyes; why then should I think upon a maid?" (Job 31:1). Do you remember what God said about Job? "There was a man in the land of Uz, whose name *was* Job; and that man was perfect and upright, and one that feared God, and eschewed evil" (Job 1:1). We see that Job, who was perfect and upright, could have struggled with this problem, but he made the decision to keep his eyes pure. If Job struggled, then other Christians and godly men can struggle too.

Let's look at an office scenario. Let's say that you're a single woman and work in a large office. An attractive man approaches your desk and asks, "What is your name?" I am guessing that when you first saw him, even though you thought him to be nice-looking, you were not sexually aroused. His looks, however, did not turn you off either. More than likely, it was when he asked your name that you first felt something internally, that tingle of excitement. Let's pretend he asks, "Are you single?" You respond, "Yes." He proceeds to tell you that you're the best-looking girl he has ever seen and he cannot believe men are not beating down the door to get a date with you.

Do you see where I am going with this? It is natural for you to desire this kind of attention from men. That is why ladies spend millions of dollars on perfume, clothes, and makeup every year. Let's imagine that every man you come into contact with did this kind of flirting with you. I am guessing your self-esteem would be heightened and you would be elated. Not a big problem, but let's say that God commanded, "You shall not feel good about yourself when a man compliments you about your good looks." How hard would it be for you to keep that command?

When men see an attractive lady, they are drawn to her. When she dresses provocatively, it is as if she is flirting with him, inviting him to engage with her. This can be especially difficult for a man who is not walking with the Lord. That is why men have to work hard at keeping their eyes to themselves.

Now let's go back to our office scenario. What if a married man is drawn to you because of your appearance, flirts with you, and begins to have lustful thoughts? He would have committed adultery in his heart. I'm reminded of the old adage, "It takes two to tango." For there to be adultery, both a woman and a man are involved. John tells us how Jesus drew attention to this fact in the Gospel of John, chapter eight. Some men brought a woman caught in adultery to Jesus. Jesus did not respond verbally to them at first. Instead, He wrote something on the ground. Notice, however, that they did not bring the man. Many Bible scholars believe that what Jesus wrote on the ground was "Where's the man?" Therefore, women, if a man commits adultery in his heart, because of the way you dress, it makes you an accessory to that sin.

Men struggle greatly with visual stimulation. It's right for them to be attracted to women, but must do so within the boundaries set by God. I like what a preacher from a strict Bible college said. At this college, boys and girls were not allowed to touch each other. The preacher said, "If you come to college and you touch a girl you'll get kicked out, but if you don't <u>want</u> to, then you'll get kicked out also!" It is a hard and serious God-given struggle for men.

In *Every Man's Battle*, the authors explain an important point that women need to understand about men. An excerpt is below.

> Men receive gratification through the eyes…Our eyes give men the means to sin

broadly and at will. We don't need a date or mistress. We don't ever need to wait. We have our eyes and can draw sexual gratification through them at any time. We're turned on by female nudity in any way, shape, or form...

Women seldom understand this because they aren't sexually stimulated in the same way. Their ignitions are tied to touch and relationship. They view this visual aspect of our sexuality as shallow and dirty, even detestable. [16]

So, to summarize this chapter, there is a big temptation for men. Women, you have a responsibility to dress in a way that only brings attention to godliness. In addition, by implication, you sin with the man you lead into sin.

.

CHAPTER FOUR

Man's Responsibility

Christian men have a great responsibility to keep their minds and hearts secured against the lust of the world. For one, we live in a godless society that does not love the Lord. We cannot expect unsaved women to be respectful of the temptations we have as Christian men.

Do you remember the verse quoted earlier from Job? "I made a covenant with mine eyes; why then should I think upon a maid?" (Job 31:1). We have to learn to secure our eyes as Job did. We must also secure our hearts and do what 1 Thessalonians 4:4 advises, "That every one of you should know how to possess his vessel in sanctification and honour."

As Christian men, we cannot use the excuse that a "woman was dressed improperly and that is the reason for my sin." We have a choice to look or not. If an impure thought pops in our minds, we are to rebuke it, think about our wives (if we are married), and responsibility to God. Our responsibility to God should always be of the utmost importance to us.

Many men will not stare at another lady in front of their wife. He may act this way because he is afraid she will see him and confront him. He may also refrain from staring at the other woman out of respect for his wife. Christian men should remember that any time they are staring at a woman, they are doing so in front of God. They are accountable to God 24/7 and God knows the lust of their hearts. Are you willing to show the same respect to God?

I know this is rather simplistic and I am not telling men anything new. There are many resources that help Christian men in this area. I highly recommend a book called, *When Good Men Are Tempted* by Bill Perkins.[17] This book will not only be of help to men in understanding temptations, but women can benefit from it as well.

What about the outward adornment? Is this just a woman's issue or are men subject to Christian guidelines in this area too? Just as the biblical principles of distinction that cover nudity (modesty) and separation from the world apply to women, they are true for men also. I believe that women are sometimes treated unfairly, even attacked with this issue, while men are given a pass.

It is true that men are affected to a greater degree by women's outward adornment, than women are affected by a man's outward appearance. However, since a vast majority of pastors, preachers, and church leaders are men, the teaching that the Church receives on this subject is usually from a man's point of view. These men may or may not be objective. Ladies may not fully understand men's struggle with lust; neither can men fully understand women's struggles with emotional attraction. This is why I have co-written this book with my wife. It is our desire to bring both perspectives to the forefront for the reader's consideration.

For men, the commands we spoke about for distinction apply to us also. Men are not to wear feminine clothes or outward adornment. The apostle Paul wrote to Timothy, "In like manner also, that women adorn themselves in modest apparel, with shamefacedness and sobriety; not with broided hair, or gold, or pearls, or costly array" (1 Timothy 2:9). This verse sheds light for men also. While these commands are given to ladies, not men, remember that I said there is a purpose behind every command. I don't believe God commanded men specifically in this verse regarding "broided hair, or gold, or pearls" because men were not to wear them. Therefore, it should not be an issue. Men were already instructed not to adorn themselves in this manner when they were told to be distinct from women in all areas of their outward adornment.

My wife and I were at a popular Bible college recently and came across a young man who was a student. He wore form-fitting blue jeans, bracelets, and more than one necklace. Our first impression was that he looked like a girl. To be truthful, he looked like a lesbian trying to look like a boy. Feminism has culturally seeped into our men because many fathers are not actively involved in the lives of their sons. Boys spend most of their time around their mothers. They naturally pick up on the mother's mannerism and femininity.

As men, we must make sure what we wear is very distinct in nature to our gender. For example, when it comes to jewelry, you don't see many men in the Bible wearing it, except for a few times where men had earrings. Those earrings, however, were always associated with the bondage of pagan captivity. Often, when the Israelites went into bondage they were branded like livestock to show that they were owned by a particular owner. For example in Exodus we read:

> And Aaron said unto them, Break off the golden earrings, which *are* in the ears of your wives, of your sons, and of your daughters, and bring *them* unto me. And all the people brake off the golden earrings which *were* in their ears, and brought *them* unto Aaron. And he received *them* at their hand, and fashioned it with a graving tool, after he had made it a molten calf: and they said, These *be* thy gods, O Israel, which brought thee up out of the land of Egypt. And when Aaron saw it, he built an altar before it; and Aaron made proclamation,

and said, To morrow *is* a feast to the LORD. (Exodus 32:2-5)

This incident with Aaron happened soon after Israel came out of Egypt, where they had been slaves. Many of the worldly ways of Egypt still prevailed in their lives. This story demonstrates how they doubted God's provisions. They took off their earrings and made them into an idol, still following pagan rituals.

The rest of the time throughout God's Word, you see men's earrings surrounded with pagan association. Other times when jewelry is mentioned, it is associated with women, not men. Therefore, I conclude that jewelry was intended primarily for women and not men. Think on what God said to Jacob and Jacob to his family when he went to Bethel. "And God said unto Jacob, Arise, go up to Bethel, and dwell there: and make there an altar unto God, that appeared unto thee when thou fleddest from the face of Esau thy brother. Then Jacob said unto his household, and to all that *were* with him, Put away the strange gods that *are* among you, and be clean, and change your garments" (Genesis 35:1-2).

What about a wedding ring on a man? We do see rings in the Bible on men. For example, the story of Esther tells us, "And the king took off his ring, which he had taken from Haman, and gave it unto Mordecai. And Esther set Mordecai over the house of Haman" (Esther 8:2). We also read in the parable of the prodigal son, "But the father said to his servants, Bring forth the best robe, and put *it* on him; and put a ring on *his* hand, and shoes on his feet" (Luke 15:22). So I don't think a ring is limited to a woman's attire. Many rings worn at one time, however, and necklaces give the impression, within today's culture, of women's adornment.

To add to the argument against men adorning themselves lavishly with rings and jewelry, remember that ladies are commanded not to be flashy with this type of adornment. I would assume the same would be true for men. As the old saying goes "What is good for the goose is good for the gander."

How about long hair on men? As I have already told you, at one time, I had hair down to my waist; therefore, I can speak from experience. I did not have long hair to attempt looking feminine. In the 1980's, long hair was a sign of rebellion and toughness. But, the connotation that my long hair resembled a woman's was still there. The Bible speaks clearly on this subject. "Doth not even nature itself teach you, that, if a man have long hair, it is a shame unto him? But if a woman have long hair, it is a glory to her: *for her* hair is given her for a covering" (1 Corinthians 11:14-15).

This verse teaches us that the Lord gave women long hair for a covering of distinction when coming to the house of God. Men were to be shorn, thus also distinct. God says that it is wrong for the two genders to cross this line. But, one may say, as I did, "Well, it says it's a shame, not a sin." Let me ask you, "Do you want to be a shame to the Lord?" The Greek word is *atimia*, which means: "disgrace—dishonour, reproach, shame, vile." [18] None of those words are what I want to be associated with me about my Christian testimony.

If we look at the next verse in 1 Corinthians, Paul says, "But if any man seem to be contentious, we have no such custom, neither the churches of God" (1 Corinthians 11:16). The context here is not of hair, but prayer, and what Paul is saying is that if a person comes to pray, and a lady's hair is cut, it will not stop her from praying. He explains that this is the way God set the mode of prayer in the temple, but short hair on a woman will not limit her prayers. Paul's explanation means we don't have to fight about this, but we should follow the example set by nature. This verse does not cancel out the truth of the nature of the distinction of hair for men and women, but signifies there is not a custom within the church about this matter of prayer.

Men's outward adornment needs to be separate from the world. Men today are greatly affected by culture. Many T-shirts advertising rock bands, rap music, and country music give a negative connotation toward women. Such clothing is associated with worldliness and Christian men should be very careful. Christians are called to "come out" and be distinct. Similarly, a woman should be recognized as being modest compared to the world—even from a distance.

What is the first impression a person gets from your dress? Is it that you're a Green Bay Packers fan or a Red Sox fan? I have always enjoyed riding motorcycles, and once took a 4,000 mile trip. Though I don't believe it is sinful to ride a motorcycle, I do have a conviction that to dress in all the leather and look like a Hell's Angels biker would be a sin for me. I would not be representing the Lord in a manner of separation from the world and distinction from the unsaved.

Christian men's attire needs to be modest, not showing off their muscles and physique, just as a woman's attire should not be used to show her figure or form. A man dressing in a way to show off his physique does so to bring glory to himself, not to God. The world tries to bring attention to itself; a Christian's dress and motive should bring attention to godliness.

When the Israelites attacked Jericho, they were instructed not to take the accursed things for themselves. Yet, one man, Achan, disobeyed. His sin brought punishment on the entire Israel nation. In the same way, one Christian dressing improperly, taking the accursed things for himself, can bring punishment upon all Christians. The reputation of all Christians is at stake when even one of us misrepresents Christ in our personal lives.

CHAPTER FIVE

Our Journey
From My Heart to Yours (Heidi)

As my husband and I have written this book, I have a few thoughts at the end that I would like to share; thoughts that really did not fit within the body of the book.

Both of us grew up in non-Christian homes. Neither set of parents taught us about distinction and modesty. The atmosphere of the home where I grew up was unsettling. I was the adopted child, and I had two older brothers of whom I wanted to fit into their world in any way I could, even if that meant being a tomboy. Also, because I was born with a facial deformity, I was unattractive to most people.

As I got older, I had a desire to grow in the Lord and be surrounded by godly people to help in my sanctification. I enrolled in and attended a reputable Christian college that I thought would provide the godly counsel I needed. There were many rules at this college with a lot of emphasis on dress. I did not have a problem with the dress code.

I wanted to enter a new world, putting my growing up years and unsettling home atmosphere behind me. I felt safe and loved by many at the college. Because of that feeling of love and security, I wanted to obey. During my college days, my spirituality grew.

Yes, I wore skirts or dresses all the time, and back then panty hose were a requirement too. It wasn't that I only obeyed with my actions and not my heart. I obeyed wholeheartedly, but I did not understand the whys of the rules. Unfortunately, we were told to be modest but not taught why. During this time, I started to associate spirituality with the way I dressed.

I stayed at that college willingly for six years, at the end receiving both a Bachelor's degree and a Master's Degree. After graduation, I moved to Virginia and taught at a solid fundamental Baptist church school, where the same dress standards from the Bible college were the adhered-to guidelines.

My husband has given you many illustrations of himself in this book, illustrations concerning his appearance and his journey to cut his hair. The first college he attended struggled with where to set their standards. As a result, there was a lot of division within the student body, administration, and the churches associated with the college. During his freshman year, the college split. My husband went the way of the more conservative side and chose a new college that better reflected his stand on these issues.

After Jerry's graduation and ordination in 2001, we moved to Wisconsin, where we plunged into leadership roles. My husband became the senior pastor and I the pastor's wife.

For the first time, I did not have a college, employer, or parent dictating what I should wear and when I should wear it. Both my husband and I felt that dresses were a woman's best attire most of the time, especially when it came to church functions. We came to this decision, mostly because that was the way it was in all the churches we had been members of or visited, and that was the way the pastors' wives for whom we had deep respect dressed. It was a logical conclusion that our belief that women should wear dresses in church was correct.

The Wisconsin church was very different from churches we had previously attended. Unbeknownst to us, only one lady and her family shared the same background and teaching on this subject as Jerry and me.

Because the norm for women's dress was pants, I stood out among the ladies in the church, which caused me to spend time soul-searching my heart. I concluded that many of my viewpoints on outward adornment had been told to me. I had not adopted them biblically for myself. Before going to college, I had no problem with wearing pants or jeans, especially when on vacation or with my family.

When we began our ministry, I did not wear pants outside the home. I did not have a personal conviction with pants as women's attire, but I wanted to set an example for others in following my husband's leadership for our church.

Meanwhile, my husband worked hard to rebuild the church attendance and set a higher standard for the ministry in our new church. He stood strong with his vision for the church, what the church should be doing, how the church could reach out, and how the church should look. He preached what he believed from his heartfelt convictions.

He publicly preached on outward adornment, Christian modesty, and distinction; however he never preached that pants were an abomination. He did preach that dresses and skirts were best for ladies, giving a good testimony for Christian modesty. He never dictated what ladies should wear outside of church or in their homes, but cautioned them on how they represented the Church and the Lord.

At that time, I did not have a guiding principle in my heart against pants; however, I respected my husband and followed him. Some ladies asked me if I had a conviction about pants. "No," I told them, "but my husband prefers me in skirts or dresses and I respect his leadership and stand."

I battled within my heart to fit in for many years, even up to writing this book. Growing up, I wanted to fit in, but struggled because of being adopted and my facial deformity. In college, I wanted to fit in, but struggled because I didn't come from a popular church or look like the popular and prestigious students of the student body. Now, we had moved away from family and friends to a church where my husband was the pastor and, once again, I felt like I didn't fit in. I was unhappy, wanted to blend in with the other ladies, and have them accept me into their heart and lives.

Over the last nine years, I learned to wholly look to my husband for leadership and to be an example of loving submission. At the same time, I sought what the Lord wanted for my life.

My husband had no problem with me wearing modest pants while at home. He wanted me to be comfortable playing with the boys, climbing over baby gates, and cleaning the house. He believed that pants were fine within the home, but if men came to the house or I went out in public that I should wear a dress or skirt.

God has been working on my heart though about what I should wear. I have learned that it's not necessarily important what I was taught in college or what I was admonished to wear by others after college. What is important is what God says in His Word and through the conviction of His Holy Spirit in MY heart! God's Word tells us, "One man esteemeth one day above another: another esteemeth every day *alike*. Let every man be fully persuaded in his own mind" (Romans 14:5).

Over the years, I have searched the Scriptures, prayed, sought godly women, and learned about modesty. My wonderful husband has allowed me to search the Lord in these areas, and has been very understanding and listening. I am very careful not to try to influence him and his convictions. I never want to be an Eve, leading my husband in the wrong direction.

I was the one that bought Nancy Leigh DeMoss' booklets on modesty. I don't know if I was looking for an excuse to wear pants or not, but I bought all the books from as many fundamental sources as I could find. I think I secretly hoped that someone would summarize what was scripturally right.

I don't think these books helped that much, because they either avoided the pants issue or they were so extreme I knew they were trying to please a certain crowd. Many of them misused Scriptures to make their point. During this time of searching, I experienced many different emotions and reactions that came with my frustrations. I knew my heart was not right concerning other people and the way they dressed. Not only did I learn to obey the dress standards in college and around other fundamental Baptists and families, I saw and acquired the judgmental attitude towards those that didn't conform. I learned by example to judge and admonish others because of what they wore to church. Because I respected my husband and his convictions regarding appropriate dress for each occasion, I expected everyone else to do the same.

Jerry never took it personally when people did not conform. There were only a couple of times that he asked me to have a lady change into a more modest attire while serving in the church. I never remember hearing him ask on any other occasion, "Did you see how that person was dressed?" or say, "They were not dressed appropriately for church." However, Jerry is like many men who really don't see how much clothing means to women or how sensitive this issue can be for them.

From early childhood, getting new clothes can be like winning the lottery for many girls. Men usually couldn't care less. For ladies it is much more personal. I can tell you that often I was the one who took the issue personally. Even though I struggled with my own personal convictions on dress, I did not handle some situations correctly regarding the viewpoints of other women.

I have recently renewed a friendship with a former teenager of our church. She is married now and does not attend our church with her family at this time. About a year ago, she told me that she was glad my husband and I came to Victory, that we've stayed over the course of years, and she's seen the fruit of our labors in the Lord.

She said she also noticed that I had changed. She's right. She reminded me of an encounter I had with her when Jerry and I first came to Victory. I didn't remember the incident, but knowing my heart back then, I believe that it played out like she said.

She said our church had a picnic, or something of that nature, and she arrived wearing shorts. Apparently I told her what she was wearing was "immodest" and "not acceptable" at church.

I don't doubt that I would have said that. That is how I was taught to treat others who did not conform to the dress standards of our college institution or other peer groups. Even visiting schools coming to the college campus had to dress according to the college standards and would be told to change by a teacher, staff person, or other person of authority and leadership.

Did I necessarily have a conviction against shorts at the time? No! Was I against jeans or pants? No! But, my brain was wired to admonish anyone at church to dress according to the standards I had been taught. If a rebuke hurt someone's feelings, the important thing at the time was that conformity was accomplished.

As I went back down memory lane with the teenager, who is now a young adult, she told me she loved me and knew I had a changed heart attitude. I am thankful that it is evident in my speech and walk that God has worked in my heart in such a way that I no longer come across as offensive to our ladies and precious teenagers. It has been a growing process.

Another avenue used by God in the process of my sanctification was the influences and examples

I've had who have grown and changed in their standards, values, and testimony.

People who I once thought were the elite of Christendom because of their high dress standards, are the same people who no longer require dresses and skirts for themselves, their wives, daughters, or granddaughters and who attend churches that have more contemporary standards than they once held. Bitterness settled into my heart when I learned that many of the people who admonished me regarding my outward adornment, taught me that godliness was in part how I dressed, and to admonish those who did not comply to their dress codes, were now dressing in the attire that just a few years ago they had judged negatively. I thought, "The whole time I was trying to fit in, be accounted as godly, judged because my clothes, hair, and background weren't good enough, and suffering years of feeling inadequate was all for nought!"

But it wasn't. The Lord used the changing testimonies of these prominent people in the flourishing years of my spiritual growth to remind me and show me that my spirituality and status before God is based on my heart and not my looks. God reminds me from His Word, "But the LORD said unto Samuel, Look not on his countenance, or on the height of his stature; because I have refused him: for *the LORD seeth* not as man seeth; for man looketh on the outward appearance, but the LORD looketh on the heart" (1 Samuel 16:7).

Also, my struggle has taught me not to compare myself to others. The Bible says, "For we dare not make ourselves of the number, or compare ourselves with some that commend themselves: but they measuring themselves by themselves, and comparing themselves among themselves, are not wise" (2 Corinthians 10:12).

Those who measure themselves, commend themselves, and compare themselves to others who don't dress like them are not wise. That includes me and the way I used to be. Now that the testimonies and principles from those I used to look up to have changed, I'm sure I'm not the only one who has looked at them with disheartenment and hurt.

With all that being said, are my standards now lower because people I highly regarded as being the spiritual elite have lowered their standards? Do I not care about modesty anymore? Have I convinced my husband that it doesn't matter what a woman, teenager, or little girl wears?

The answers are emphatically "No!" I have not lowered my standards, but have sought the Lord with my whole heart, not half-heartedly looking for justification of my preferences. I can honestly say that God has raised my standards! Do I think loose-fitting pants, or loose-fitting, knee-length shorts are sinful? No! As you've read earlier in this book, my husband and I believe there is a time and place for certain attire, and that is what we adhere to. Yes, I care about modesty—more than ever— because

God has put that desire in my heart personally. It does not come from an institution, or my husband, or anyone else. And, no, I was not convinced of my change of heart by my husband or anything he wrote in this book. In fact, I told him how the Lord has worked on my heart through the writing of this book to bring me to my own convictions and preferences regarding modesty. To be honest, I was not ready to co-author this book with him when I knew in my heart I wasn't wholeheartedly in agreement with him in everything on this subject. For years, I happily agreed in subjection to his preferences, convictions, and standards for the church and our family, but those standards were not from my heart. How could I write a book on the subject when I felt like that?

Jerry has worked on this book by himself for some time. I am so thankful that he approached me about us co-authoring the book. Through the process of writing, I finally had to deal with this issue straight on. I have had to listen to the Lord, listen to the Spirit's guidance, honestly hear what He said to me, and submit to what I hear.

Psalm 139 says, "Search me, O God, and know my heart: try me, and know my thoughts: And see if *there be any* wicked way in me, and lead me in the way everlasting" (Psalm 139:23-24). I like to paraphrase that as, "Lord search my heart and know my thoughts; make sure that I am not seeking to only hear what I want to hear and not what You have for my life."

Another favorite verse of mine is from Psalm 143: "Teach me to do thy will; for thou *art* my God: thy spirit is good; lead me into the land of uprightness" (Psalm 143:10). Again, I paraphrase that verse as, "Teach me, Lord, Your will for my life. Not what others think, say, or do, but what You want for me. I want to live holy and acceptable unto You and You only."

Because of these verses, and because God worked in me personally, I now have firm convictions from my heart. God let me see that convictions regarding modesty are a matter of the heart and are not manmade. Early in my life, what I saw and gleaned from others was not the Spirit's leading, but man's rules. Rules are fine, and necessary in church, institutions, work environments, restaurants, etc., but we as Christians also need to be persuaded from our hearts to live these rules unto God and not unto man.

I no longer bat my eye at ANY lady who wears slacks or jeans to church. My husband sets the standard for those teaching, singing, and serving. He asks them to dress according to church guidelines while on duty at church.

The Lord works on His children from the inside out, just as He did for me. It took me nine years to build my convictions between me and the Lord when it comes to modesty. I cannot judge someone else if they are honestly seeking His will. I will, however, warn others with a verse from Romans, "*There* is therefore now no condemnation to them which are in Christ Jesus, who walk not after the flesh, but after the Spirit" (Romans 8:1). Though I sought the Lord's answers, I walked after people that I looked up to. At the same time, I selfishly hoped and looked for answers from books, the Bible, and God's Spirit. I searched for answers that justified my preferences; therefore, I was walking after the flesh, trying to find something or someone who agreed with me about wearing jeans, pants, or shorts outside of church. I searched because I hadn't heard yea or nay from the Lord on the issue. Finally, God revealed the answers for me within my own heart.

So if a Christian lady now comes to me questioning her attire and asking my opinion, I can answer, "When looking in the mirror, are you pleasing God or man? Literally." I can refer them to the book of Matthew, "Ye are the light of the world. A city that is set on an hill cannot be hid. Neither do men light a candle, and put it under a bushel, but on a candlestick; and it giveth light unto all that are in the house. Let your light so shine before men, that they may see your good works, and glorify your Father which is in heaven" (Matthew 5:14-16).

As Christians, we are God's light to a lost and dying world. Does my attire bring glory to the Lord? When people see me, does my appearance reflect my testimony for God, or does my appearance distract them from the things of God?

I praise God that He is forever merciful and full of grace for His children. It took me nine years to surrender my will and preferences regarding dress standards for my personal and public life.

I always thought I was modest and did not purposely wear clothes to attract other men, but neither did I understand what men really notice about women. Because I felt unattractive due to the right side of my face and my small right eye, I was unaware of what really tempts a man until I studied God's Word, surrendered, and found the answers.

I know there are thousands who have experienced some of the same struggles I have. They grew up in a strict Christian home, attended a stringent college, plunged into the world on their own, and faced rules and standards that were not in their hearts. The journeys of many ladies have taken them in a sad direction. Many of them have nothing to do with church today. They flounder in their convictions concerning outward adornment. Others have continued with a harsh spirit held over from rigid upbringings or pharisaical churches. They sit among church members with the same critical spirit I once followed and pushed onto others.

If there is ever a time when a book is needed like this one, it is now. As we've been writing this book, we went out to a restaurant the other day. I watched cute teenage waitresses walk around in their low-ride jeans and T-shirts and it dawned on me, "Wow! They look sexy!" Their clothes asked men and women to follow them with their eyes. I sat at our table, with my new knowledge and convictions from the Lord and tried to view those teenage girls through the eyes of a man. It was a real prompting of the Holy Spirit. I saw tight jeans and T-shirts, skinny bodies, and the shape of their hips, waist, and chest. I was not drawn to any form of godliness or worship of my Savior. I wondered, "How many men in this restaurant are lusting after these girls because they flaunt their figures before them?" The "sexy" look of these teenagers broke my heart. Their outer adornment cried out, "Look at me! I'm thin, attractive, and flaunting it for the entire world to see!" I was grieved knowing that adultery of the heart was very present around me.

I want to thank you for reading my personal journey in this last chapter. I pray God will use this book and my testimony to lead you and other women who are searching to find God's leading regarding your dress standards. I pray you find answers that are honoring to Him and not to self or others. As God speaks, may you not ignore the Lord as I once did, or neglect to seek Him wholeheartedly. Be ready to obey what He tells you!

Our purpose in life as Christians is to do all for the glory of God, whether we are eating, drinking, dressing with a purpose, or living out our daily lives. We are not to be a stumbling block or judge others that may not live as we do. In all things our goal is to reach people for Christ through our testimony, that they will be saved and, spend eternity with our Lord and Savior Jesus Christ.

I leave you with some verses from 1 Corinthians, "Whether therefore ye eat, or drink, or whatsoever ye do, do all to the glory of God. Give none offence, neither to the Jews, nor to the Gentiles, nor to the church of God: Even as I please all *men* in all *things*, not seeking mine own *profit*, but the profit of many, that they may be saved" (1 Corinthians 10:31-33).

CONCLUSION

The Lord is concerned about what Christians wear because we are dressing the temple of God (our bodies), and He will use us in a mighty way if we will allow Him. There are four different principles from the Bible that should guide us when making a decision concerning the clothes we select and our overall appearance. Four questions you can ask yourself are:

1. Does my clothing cover my nudity?
2. Do I represent distinction between the genders?
3. Am I dressed in a way that separates me from the world?
4. What is the purpose of the clothes I select when I am dressing?

This book has given you different arguments about various forms of modern clothing and how they relate to these four principles.

We have seen that God does not specifically give us a "thou shalt not wear" command when it comes to specific clothing, but because the Bible is a Living Book, that is applicable to all ages, cultures, and generations, the Lord gives us principles that can guide us, regardless of our culture.

Our attire and dress are spiritual decisions every Christian must make. One day you will give an account to the Lord concerning your modesty, distinction, purpose of your clothing, and whether or not you have been a stumbling block to others. If you agree with me when Jesus uses the words "with her" when describing lustful adultery of the heart, you may wonder how many ladies have committed adultery by their manner of dress. All of us, men and women, will give an account to the Lord as to whether or not we have separated ourselves from pagan culture.

All of this accountability will happen at the Judgment Seat of Christ, which will determine our rewards from the Lord that we have earned and will put at the feet of Him. I Corinthians 3:12-17 says,

> Now if any man build upon this foundation gold, silver, precious stones, wood, hay, stubble; Every man's work shall be made manifest: for the day shall declare it, because it shall be revealed by fire; and the fire shall try every man's work of what sort it is. If any man's work abide which he hath built thereupon, he shall receive a reward. If any man's work shall be burned, he shall suffer loss: but he himself shall be saved; yet so as by fire. Know ye not that ye are the temple of God, and *that* the Spirit of God dwelleth in you? If any man defile the temple of God, him shall God destroy; for

the temple of God is holy, which *temple* ye
are.

These verses teach that Christians have a
responsibility to labor for the Lord with the right
motive and methods so we don't lose our reward.
All the works that are done incorrectly because of
motive or disobedience will be burned up. Those
things that were done pleasing to the Lord will
stand the test of judgment. What is very interesting
is the last part of the verses. It says, "Know ye not
that ye are the temple of God, and that the Spirit of
God dwelleth in you? If any man defile the temple
of God, him shall God destroy; for the temple of
God is holy, which *temple* ye are" (1 Corinthians
3:16-17). I think this adds emphasis that a part of
this judgment will focus on our outward as well as
inward temple. May God lead, guide, and direct
you as you seek what is His will for your life when
it comes to your attire.

Going back to the illustration from chapter one,
where the young Christian woman, Brenda, was
faced with the issue of pants, I stated that all parties
were wrong. The church should have taught its
members what God's Word says on this subject.
Perhaps a book, like this one, to refer the young
Christian to, rather than having the unbalanced
and biblically incorrect lady being their spokesperson, could have been helpful. The church had
every right to set the standard for their teachers,
but they, and Mr. Smith, should have backed it up

with Scripture and reasons why they chose this path. I would guess that if they had chosen the uniform approach and/or stumbling block argument, things might have turned out very different.

The church spokesperson, Mrs. Johnson, made her comments out of biblical ignorance and should have studied the issue more or referred the young Christian back to the leadership. And our young Christian, Brenda, should have realized that what she wore was not under judgment from the ladies, but God. She was guilty of allowing Satan to use misinformation against her, and convince her to leave a church that was probably the will of God for her. She also could have been more respectful of the other woman's convictions and stand, as she probably was respectful in retail stores, restaurants, and other places that require certain dress attire.

ENDNOTES

[1] Inspired by illustration from Ketchum, Lance, PhD., *Parenting a Soul*, (Hutchinson, Minnesota, Disciple Maker Ministry) p. 243

[2] DeMoss, Nancy Leigh, *The Look: Does God Really Care What I Wear?* (Buchanan, MI: Life Action 2003) p. 12

[3] *Wikipedia,The Free Encyclopedia*, (Wikimedia Foundation, Inc. Website: n.d.) http://en.wikipedia.org/wiki/Culottes

[4] *Wikipedia,The Free Encyclopedia*, (Wikimedia Foundation, Inc. Website: n.d.) http://en.wikipedia.org/wiki/Culottes

[5] *A Dictionary of the Holy Bible*, (American Tract Society, 1859)

[6] Unidentified source.

[7] *Vine's Expository Dictionary*

[8] DeMoss, Nancy Leigh, *The Look: Does God Really Care What I Wear?* (Buchanan, MI: Life Action 2003) p. 13

[9] Douglas, J. D., *Zondervan's Pictorial Bible Dictionary*, (Zondervan, September, 1988)

[10] *Christians and Sex*, Christianity Today Leadership Journal, (March, 2005)

[11] The London School of Economics, 2002

[12] *Focus on the Family* poll, (Oct. 1, 2003)

[13] Barna Group

[14] Comsearch Media Matrix

[15] *Focus on the Family* poll, (Oct. 1, 2003)

[16] Arterburn, Steve and Stocker, Fred with Yorkey, Mike, *Every Man's Battle* (Colorado Springs: Waterbrook Press, 2000) pp. 65-66

[17] Perkins, Bill, *When Good Men are Tempted*, (Zondervan, August 2007)

[18] Strong, James, *Strong's Concordance*, (Madison, N.J.)

LaVergne, TN USA
30 May 2010
184481LV00001B/2/P